Praise for *The Disaster* ...

"A wall-to-wall handbook for how to conduct yourself before, during, and after any number of wide-scale disasters. . . . An impressively thorough resource that belongs in any disaster-prep kit. *The Disaster Survival Bible* has definitely earned its easily accessible place on my bookshelf. Right by the door. Just in case."

—*San Francisco Book Review*

"When we do not experience disasters or see them in our neighborhoods, we forget to prepare for them. Yet preparedness can make the difference between staying alive and perishing. . . . *The Disaster Survival Bible* is very thorough and covers in great detail every aspect of potential disasters."

—*Portland Book Review*

Praise for *Stop Being a Victim*

"Voltaire wrote that common sense isn't so common. But thank goodness in this day and age we have guys like Junius Podrug to give us all a good measure of it in *Stop Being a Victim*."

—David Hagberg, *New York Times* bestselling author of *Castro's Daughter*

"Your survival kit for the new millennium . . . [T]his book is more than crucial to your well-being. It is indispensible to your staying alive."

—Jack Anderson, Pulitzer Prize-winning columnist

"*Stop Being a Victim* is witty, readable, filled with fascinating anecdotes, real flesh-and-blood people, and electrifying examples of both what to do and what not to do. It might just help us all survive the twenty-first century."

—Gerald W. Gibbs, author of *The Complete Guide to Credit and Loans*

"A true survival manual for the new millennium."

—R. J. Pineiro, author of *Y2K*

THE
DISASTER
SURVIVAL
BIBLE

Junius Podrug

A Tom Doherty Associates Book
New York

THE DISASTER SURVIVAL BIBLE

Copyright © 2012 by Junius Podrug

A Forge Book
Published by Tom Doherty Associates, LLC
175 Fifth Avenue
New York, NY 10010

www.tor-forge.com

Forge® is a registered trademark of Tom Doherty Associates, LLC.

The Library of Congress has cataloged the hardcover edition as follows:

Podrug, Junius.
    The disaster survival bible / Junius Podrug. — 1st ed.
        p. cm.
    "A Tom Doherty Associates book."
    ISBN 978-0-7653-1394-2 (hardcover)
    ISBN 978-1-4668-0670-2 (e-book)
    1. Emergency management.   2. Crime prevention.   3. Security
systems.   4. Crime prevention.   I. Title.
    HD49.P63 2012
    613.6'9—dc23

                                                    2012024906

        ISBN 978-0-7653-1395-9 (trade paperback)

Forge books may be purchased for educational, business, or
promotional use. For information on bulk purchases, please contact
Macmillan Corporate and Premium Sales Department at 1-800-221-7945,
extension 5442, or write specialmarkets@macmillan.com.

First Edition: December 2012
First Trade Paperback Edition: January 2014

Printed in the United States of America

0 9 8 7 6 5 4 3 2 1

ACKNOWLEDGMENTS

While the author's name goes prominently on a book, it takes a great number of people in publishing houses and booksellers to make a book happen. Unfortunately, the nature of the trade is that most of them stay anonymous to the public. However, in this case, I want to thank editors Bob Gleason, Whitney Ross, and Kelly Quinn for their efforts in making this book happen.

AUTHOR'S NOTE

The *Are You Ready* guide from the Federal Emergency Management Agency (FEMA) is very comprehensive, literally covering all imaginable disasters short of the end of the world. The length and technical language of this guide, however, makes it less accessible than one would wish. I have added my own ideas and experiences in being prepared for surviving disasters and have streamlined as much as I could the extensive FEMA materials.

By keeping this book in your grab-and-go bag or stay-put survival kit, you will have a hard copy readily available to consult when the need arises.

CONTENTS

1. Surviving Is a Lonely Business *17*

2. The Survival Instinct *22*

3. How Secure Are We? *28*

4. Surviving on Your Own *31*

5. The Will to Survive *33*

6. A Dangerous World *38*

7. Biological Agents *40*

8. Chemical Agents *44*

9. Radiological Hazards *49*

10. Nuclear Terrorism *57*

11. Survival Tactics *59*

12. The Escape Zone *61*

13. The Safe Room *67*

14. Emergency Survival Supplies *71*

15. Vehicle Survival Kit *84*

16. Protective Masks *89*

CONTENTS

17. KI: Potassium Iodide *92*

18. Emergency Electronics *101*

19. Federal Security Guides *103*

Are You Ready? *107*

**ARE YOU READY TO SURVIVE...
ON YOUR OWN?**
We must have the tools and plans *to make it on
our own*, at least for a period of time, no
matter where we are when disaster strikes.

◀ Homeland Security Warning ▶

> **BOTTLES OF WINE RESERVED FOR GUESTS — 4**
>
> **BOTTLES OF WATER RESERVED FOR EMERGENCY — 0**

◀ Ready New York sign on subway ▶

THE

DISASTER SURVIVAL BIBLE

SURVIVING IS A
LONELY BUSINESS

An expression I heard as a kid, which I suspect came out of the Old West, is that we all have to kill our own snakes. I take it to mean that we have to handle our own problems because we can't rely upon anyone else. Of course, we cannot personally take care of all of the problems that life throws at us, but when it comes to surviving disasters, all of us have a duty to be prepared.

By their very nature, natural disasters such as hurricanes and earthquakes and disasters caused by terrorist attacks with chemical, biological, or nuclear devices are widespread occurrences that hinder and sometimes totally cripple rescue agencies.

Surviving more localized emergencies like fires and terrorist attacks requires an immediate response by us rather than waiting for the police, fire department, or emergency medical technicians (EMTs) to save us.

Since rescue agencies may be crippled or the danger may have occurred too quickly for outside help to reach us in time, we all need to be prepared to take care of ourselves.

This guide to dealing with the often insane ravages of man

and nature is based upon my own experiences coping with crimes committed against me and those close to me, the thousands of criminals I dealt with as a criminal defense lawyer, and the times I have had to deal with angry Mother Nature.

In my own mind, one of my best qualifications for giving advice is that I am paranoid—a mind-set that makes me avoid anything higher than the tenth floor of hotels because fire ladders don't reach any higher, and the first floor of motels because the bottom floor is the most easily accessible to criminals.

I do not believe that the government is completely capable of taking care of me in a crisis, and that means I have a ready-to-go plan and a stocked survival kit. I also follow a nuclear warfare preparation mentality that advises keeping at least a half tank of gas in my car at all times—advice my brother failed to heed and thus couldn't get quickly out of town when a trainload of military munitions began exploding near his neighborhood. He survived, but it's the sort of experience that can eat a piece of your soul.

While the government tends to handle large crises poorly, many governmental agencies are excellent sources of information about surviving a disaster. One of the best and most comprehensive is the publication *Are You Ready?*, from the Federal Emergency Management Agency (FEMA). However, as you would expect from a governmental agency, the very long (over two hundred single-spaced pages) guide also has information overload and often speaks in technical language.

Because the guide is valuable, I have included it as a significant part of this survival manual, and have gone through it and removed some verbiage that I feel increases the difficulty of grasping survival tips from it.

In addition, because large-scale emergencies commonly result in the loss of electrical power and an inability to access the Internet, including the FEMA guide in this book means it is readily available to you wherever you are in an emergency, as long as this book is in your survival kit.

Included at the end of my reflections on surviving are lists of governmental and nongovernmental entities that are good sources of materials on surviving a crisis—but again, survival is a lonely business and those online sources may not be available during a crisis.

Dealing personally with emergencies is discussed below in the chapter called Surviving on Your Own.

Can you benefit from reading about surviving a disaster?

The point about survival being a personal snake to deal with is emphasized not just by me but by governmental agencies: During a disaster, whether it be a terrorist attack, angry Mother Nature, or a man-made disaster such as a chemical or nuclear reactor contagion, *there will be a time during which you and your family have to survive on your own.*

That is the message, the *warning,* from every agency that has assessed the threats from terrorism and other disasters.

You must have the tools and plans to make it on your own, at least for a period of time. The rule of thumb being used by the security agencies is that you should have a grab-and-go bag (to grab as you go for your car) that will last you at least three days, and a shelter-at-home two-week supply.

Most people assume there will be a police officer, fireman, emergency medical tech, and Red Cross shelter staff at their elbow when disaster strikes. By not purchasing and storing emergency supplies, they act as if people who work in groceries and drugstores are going to leave their families and put themselves into danger to open store doors.

Don't plan on it. The ultimate responsibility for your survival falls on your shoulders. That is what the government charged with protecting you is telling you. As Harry Truman would have put it, the buck stops with each of us.

Consider this: A suitcase-size atomic bomb exploding on Wall Street in New York or in the National Mall area of Washington, DC, would rip the heart out of this country's well-being. But even short of a staggering blow against the integrity of the nation itself—the wet dream of terrorists—there are numerous city-devastating scenarios involving nuclear power plants, subway systems, chemical and biological facilities, and sporting arenas that could take place.

There is a threat to you if you live in a city; if you are within fifty or even one hundred miles from a nuclear power plant; if there's a chemical or biological facility, an oil refinery, rail tracks that carry train cars, or freeways that carry tanker trucks in the region; if you attend sporting events, gamble in a casino, drive over a bridge, live at or near a port where ships dock, fly in a commercial airliner . . . etc., etc.

In other words, if you live and breathe in this nation or even on this planet, you probably are in a danger zone where you could be subject to an attack.

That doesn't mean there are terrorists lurking near your city's water reservoir, waiting to pour a vial of toxic bacteria in the water supply. Or that you have to keep an eye out for a suspicious-looking van when you're driving across a bridge. It just means that there is a new breed of supercrime in this world, and you need to have an awareness of it and have a personal security plan to deal with it.

Most of us believe the police are our main line of protection against crime—but we still lock our doors at night, don't leave valuable items outside, and invest in security systems. We don't do that because we expect to get murdered in our beds every night—we make these simple security plans for the possibility that sometime during our lifetime, a locked door, a big dog, or an alarm company sign on our lawn may save our lives.

Federal statistics indicate that disasters disrupt hundreds of thousands of lives each year, including killing and injuring people, making natural and man-made calamities more likely to harm you than even violent crimes.

The security measures you need to take in regard to a possible emergency are easier and less time consuming than even the simple things mentioned above that protect you from more conventional crimes. The measures are most often one-time preparations, in which you arm yourself with the knowledge of what to do and make a few relatively inexpensive purchases to have the necessary "security" devices.

And it doesn't matter a great deal whether the emergency is a man-made or a natural disaster, the basic items you need and your mental processes are pretty much the same.

Is it really possible to learn a few simple tactics that can save your life when you are suddenly confronted by a life-threatening act of terrorism, an accident, or Mother Nature with a vengeance?

Yes. Absolutely. For people with a will to survive, the simple tactics outlined in this book can make the difference.

The most important trait you need in order to protect yourself is the will to survive.

2

THE SURVIVAL
INSTINCT

Everyone has a "survival instinct." But most people do not have a finely honed survival instinct that can carry them to safety during emergencies.

While no one has to be told to get out of a burning building, only a small minority of people take a second to look to where the exits are when they enter a high-rise building, a theater, a hotel, or a nightspot for the first time.

Locating the exits is a habit of those people who have finely honed survival instincts. It takes no effort, no serious thought or planning on our part—but once we have the habit of locating where the exits are (most of the time it's just a matter of a quick glance), our chances of survival during a man-made or natural disaster soar.

This book provides: (1) common-sense tactics that can save your life and the lives of your loved ones; (2) simple-to-follow instructions that can prepare you at home, work, or school for most emergencies; and (3) an easy-to-use checklist that will guide you in making your living and working environment safer in the event of a life-or-death crisis.

It also takes the enormous amount of "survival" information published by governmental security agencies, like the Department of Homeland Security (DHS) and FEMA, and explains and simplifies the material so the information can be easily used.

Most of us have an "emergency plan" for some of the contingencies in our lives—we have some savings in case of illness or loss of employment and a retirement plan for the future. But for disasters, most people have little more than a smoke detector in their bedroom and a spare tire in their car.

Sixty years ago, when the only significant threat to our national security was thermonuclear warfare with the Soviet Union, that was perhaps about all we needed. As incredible as it may sound, during the nearly five decades when atomic sabers were rattled between Americans and Soviets it was a far safer world for the average person than it is now in the post-9/11 age of terrorism and rogue nuclear states.

Why was the world safer when the Cold War produced enough nuclear weapons to destroy the entire planet several times over?

It was safer because the weapons were in the hands of rational people who had something to lose if the weapons were used.

Everyone, from the person pushing the button in a missile silo to the Soviet leadership in the Kremlin, understood that they, too, would die if the "balloon went up" (that was an expression from conventional warfare that came to be used in regard to launching atomic warfare).

One thing that has radically changed is that many of the "button pushers" and leaders today are suicidal crazies who are not only willing, but sometimes eager, to die for their cause. Or at the very least, they are capable of getting others to die for their cause.

What is most incredible is that these insane murderers are not uneducated or from the dregs of society. The 9/11 perpetrators, for the most part, spoke two or more languages. They tended to be intelligent, well educated, and technologically sophisticated—extremely dangerous traits when combined with the fact they were also mass murderers with suicidal death wishes. They were driven by hate, fantasies, and fanaticism.

Their living counterparts are not the type of people who are going to strap explosives around their waist and get on a crowded bus, or load a bomb under the seat of their car and drive into a crowded area in hopes of killing a dozen people. Instead, they are going to strike exactly as their "brothers" did before—using a complex, highly technical plot that will create massive damage and perhaps undermine the superstructure of our political or economic system.

Perhaps even more dangerous than terrorists who have to travel thousands of miles to harm us are the ones that may be living next door—the homegrown variety like Timothy McVeigh, who killed or injured nearly a thousand people with the Oklahoma City federal building bombing.

These fanatics cannot be expected to act "rationally" as most of our enemies have done in the recent past. There is nothing that will stop them from trying to kill us except killing them first. The problem is that fanaticism grows like a cancer; once it metastasizes, it is almost impossible to kill.

The question is not whether we should prepare for future terror attacks, but what type of preparation we, as individuals, should do in case we are attacked.

That does not mean we should panic or even worry about it. If we have a healthy outlook on life, we do not worry about fires, traffic accidents, or even our health—we simply take ordinary precautions to protect ourselves from these sorts of contingencies.

The same is true of accidental and intentional disasters that threaten our well-being today. We need to take ordinary precautions to protect ourselves from these new contingencies.

The second major change that has occurred is that many stockpiles of weapons of mass destruction—from chemical plants and nuclear reactors to "suitcase nukes" (small atomic bombs that can be carried to a detonation site by car)—are no longer under the

complete control of civilized governments. The collapse of the Soviet Union left that nation's nuclear facilities hemorrhaging weapons of mass destruction—there have been hundreds of incidents of
bomb-grade uranium being sold on the black market and reports
that dozens of suitcase nukes are missing.

Added to the insanity is the proliferation of nuclear weapons
by rogue states like Iran and North Korea, as well as by individual Islamic fundamentalists. No scenario of terrorism is more
chilling than the discovery that the scientist who is called the
father of Pakistan's atomic bomb program went to Afghanistan
and had secret talks with Osama bin Laden about al-Qaeda obtaining nuclear weapons.

Our parents were fortunate in another significant way during
the Cold War: Civilians were not the designated target of our enemies.

Not so anymore. Civilians are the target of choice for terrorists—
that is the express message Osama bin Laden gave to his follow-
ers. And their success at murdering over three thousand innocent
people during the 9/11 attacks has not satisfied their bloodlust,
but increased it. They now know they can do more than kill a
dozen people on a bus with a suicide bomber. They are not stupid—
they have read the reports that had one of the 9/11 planes crashed
into a nuclear reactor or chemical tank, the casualties could potentially have been in the hundreds of thousands.

Anyone in this country who thinks they are safe from the intentional—or accidental—release of radiological or chemical
toxins has not been heeding the warnings of the government.
There is one major thing that we should all realize about agencies like FEMA and Homeland Security: For political reasons,
they tend to understate threats rather than overstate them.

If you are still under the impression that an atomic bomb is
a complex device that must be delivered by a superpower in a
bomber, you still have a Cold War mentality. The atomic bombs
our security people are worried about are more likely to come to
the capital or a metro area in a van or the back of a truck.

When the government puts out repeated warnings not only

that terrorist plans have been uncovered concerning major nuclear and chemical threats but that an accident caused by human and machine error—such as those that occurred in the nuclear power plant disaster in Ukraine and the incredibly deadly Union Carbide chemical release in India—can happen here with catastrophic results over an enormous area, we should start asking ourselves what we need to do to protect ourselves and our families.

President Obama has stated that the most serious threat to America is a nuclear attack by terrorists.

The terrorists know that is the ultimate weapon and there is clear evidence that the late bin Laden and his terrorist network have tried to obtain a nuclear weapon to use against us.

"Killing Americans and their allies—civilian or military—is an individual duty for every Muslim . . . We—with God's help—call on every Muslim who believes in God and wishes to be rewarded to comply with God's order to kill the Americans and plunder their money wherever and whenever they find it."

◄| Osama bin Laden, 1998* |►

*Said before U.S. Navy SEALs brought home to him that those who live by the sword, die by the sword

How Secure
Are We?

Anyone who has an "it won't happen to me" attitude should take the following facts to heart.

- The U.S. Army Surgeon General has estimated that over two million people could be killed or injured by a terrorist attack on an American chemical plant.

- The Environmental Protection Agency (EPA) has identified 123 chemical plants in the United States where an accidental or deliberate discharge would threaten more than a million people, and 7,605 plants that threaten a thousand or more people.

- In a scenario shockingly similar to Russia's "loose nukes," where investigators have been able to casually walk out with atomic bomb–grade uranium because of lax security, U.S. investigations have revealed there is little or no security at American chemical plants, often finding gates unlocked or even wide open.

- The three greatest chemical-radiological disasters in history occurred in the last three decades.

The first was the accidental rupture of a single chemical plant tank at a Union Carbide facility in Bhopal, India, in 1984 that killed, by some estimates, twenty thousand people and severely injured hundreds of thousands more. What began as equipment failure was aggravated by human error.

The second was the accidental meltdown at the Chernobyl nuclear power plant in Ukraine in 1986 that may be the cause of as many as forty thousands deaths with hundreds of thousands more people severely injured. What began as equipment failure was aggravated by human error.

The third was the Fukushima Daiichi nuclear disaster in 2011 that resulted in the largest release of radioactive particles since Chernobyl twenty-five years earlier. The accident occurred after an earthquake-generated tsumani caused power failures at the multi-reactor site. The most frightening aspect of the disaster is how quickly and easily everything went to hell. The plants generate cooling water to keep their hot radioactive core from overheating and going out of control. When the power grid was knocked down by Mother Nature and water couldn't be pumped, the reactors overheated and went out of control. Total damage to human life and the environment will not be known for years, perhaps even decades because one major effect is cancer that can take years to develop, but the Japanese government has admitted that the disaster dangerously raised radioactive levels over thirty miles from the site.

There are millions of people, myself included, who live that close to a nuclear power plant. Which makes me wonder what is going through the minds of terrorists and other varieties of crazies now that they realize a major disaster could be triggered simply by knocking down the power grid feeding a nuclear power plant.

- The nuclear reactor meltdown at Three Mile Island near Harrisburg, Pennsylvania, caused a radiological release into the atmosphere. It was not catastrophic but threatened to become so. And again: What began as equipment failure was aggravated by human error.

- Since the fall of the Soviet Union and the collapse of its security at atomic bomb facilities, there have been dozens of thefts of bomb-grade uranium and reports of missing suitcase nukes.

This list doesn't include natural disasters like Hurricanes Katrina and Irene that caused untold damage and hardships.

These security facts should chill to the bone everyone in this country who has any common sense. After reading them, I have come to the conclusion that the paranoia I have always been afflicted with is nothing more than a sense of heightened awareness of the dangerous world we live in.

SURVIVING ON
YOUR OWN

Emergencies are not planned events. We are not given time to prepare before disaster strikes. Most survival decisions have to be made quickly—reaction time may be no more than seconds, if that.

But the "survival instinct" that kicks in when we need it is nothing more than learned behavior; there are a few common-sense rules we need to know. These simple rules apply to most of the potential disaster situations—terrorist, accidental, and even natural phenomena—that we are likely to encounter.

One of the main rules is nothing more than what you are doing at this moment: Get advice on how to cope with emergencies before they occur and it is too late.

Since 9/11, we have been inundated with frightening scenarios of the dangers that may confront us. Alarming words describing types of disasters—*biological, chemical, radiological, nuclear*—have become buzzwords in our vocabulary.

But the threats are real—and as the statistics quoted earlier in the How Secure Are We? chapter demonstrate, the disaster scenarios are even worse than the vast majority of people in this country realize.

It doesn't matter whether the threat to us is biological, chemical, radiological, or nuclear, or even whether it is created by accident or intentionally. The issue is *how* to survive a disaster of widespread proportions that comes about accidentally through human and/or machine error, or intentionally through the acts of terrorists and crazies.

Even though the governmental publications do not make this point, when we examine the disaster scenarios and our survival tactics, we will see that *the actions to be taken are basically the same regardless of the nature of the emergency.*

IS THERE ALWAYS A SNAKE IN PARADISE?

It seems like every time we get rid of one threat to world peace, another raises its ugly head.

- We defeated the Nazis and the Cold War erupted from the threat of atomic warfare with the Soviet Union.
- The Evil Empire collapsed, leaving behind a thousand unguarded loose nuke sites in the former Soviet states . . . about the same time a hideous demon called terrorism was born.
- The death of Osama bin Laden was a blow against terrorism, but not its defeat.

In the 1960s, a stunning premise for Armageddon was a situation in which atomic warfare was started by equipment failure compounded by human error.

The nightmare of our era is a catastrophic clash between good and evil, a battle of biblical proportions, but not one that will take place on a battlefield—it would more likely begin with a suicide bomber approaching a chemical or nuclear plant, or even detonating a suitcase nuke in a populated area.

The only significant difference between the insane lone murderers we call "serial killers" and the insane mass murderers we call "terrorists" is that serial killers attack one victim at a time . . .

THE WILL TO
SURVIVE

Absent blind luck, surviving a disaster requires *knowledge* and *preparation*. People who have acquired the knowledge and done the preparation have a crucial trait: a heightened will to survive.

People die every day in situations where there is no chance of survival. There is nothing we can do about those situations. When I was a kid, people had a fatalistic attitude about life—they said when it was your time, you went. Many people still think that way, and don't bother to buckle their seatbelts no matter how many accident studies show that safety belts save lives.

People with a will to survive may believe that when it's their time, they will have to go . . . but they will do everything in their power to avoid it being "their time." My attitude is that I will go kicking and screaming and fighting all the way. And that seems to be the same attitude as other people who have a highly developed sense of survival and who never gave up—people have cut off their own limbs to free themselves from being trapped, drunk their own urine, survived the savage sea, crossed trackless deserts and impenetrable jungles.

Obviously, not all disasters are survivable. But if there is a chance, we should be as mentally and physically prepared to do whatever is necessary to get ourselves, our families, and those around us out of harm's way.

We all have that will to survive, that urge to get out of the burning building. But some of us have a better developed sense of it than others. It's something akin to what they say about fighting: It's not the dog in the fight, but the fight in the dog.

The fact that you are reading this book, getting prepared mentally, and, I hope, planning to follow through with a few basics to be physically prepared in terms of a few inexpensive supplies, shows that you have a heightened will to survive.

The person who checks for the locations of the fire escapes nearest his hotel room before going to sleep has an infinitely better chance of surviving a fire than the person who has to find the stairwell in blinding, choking smoke.

If you are in a situation that demands action, the difference between people who are prepared and those who stand around in a confused daze is often the difference between living and dying.

The will to survive is a frame of mind. We all have it to some extent or another. We already have a daily routine that keeps us safe—we look both ways before we cross a street, drive a car equipped with seatbelts, have smoke detectors in our residence, and stay away from ATMs in bad neighborhoods at night (or any other time if we can avoid it).

Those are just a few of the survival tactics we learned over our lifetimes, starting with childhood lessons about looking both ways before crossing a street and not talking to strangers, and adding onto our knowledge of survival techniques as we grew older.

We don't live in a world with the same contingencies as the one we were born in. Not only has the threat of foreign and home-grown terrorism come along like a snake in paradise after the fall of the Soviet Union, but we have entered an age of extreme weather fed by global warming that unleashes unparalleled violence and an era of corporate greed, irresponsibility, and bureaucratic incompetence, which makes us unsafe from the chemical or nuclear plant down the street.

A Homeland Security statement makes a good point in dealing with the contingencies of the new world order that we live in:

PREPARING MAKES SENSE

The likelihood of you and your family surviving a house fire depends as much on having a working smoke detector and an exit strategy as on a well-trained fire department.

The same is true for surviving a terrorist attack. We must have the tools and plans to *make it on our own,* at least for a period of time, no matter where we are when disaster strikes. Just like having a working smoke detector, preparing for the unexpected makes sense. Get ready now.

Make it on our own. It's a phrase each of us needs to drill into our heads. There are no disaster scenarios in which you will have a policeman, a fireman, and a medical expert standing at your side when it hits. The best you can hope for is a response sometime after the disaster strikes.

How long will you have to wait for a response? That will depend on the situation; it may be minutes, hours, or even days. There are tragic situations, like the 9/11 attacks, in which the emergency response teams were not only helpless because of the nature of the disasters, but the courageous emergency response personnel themselves became victims.

In the case of the accidental release of a radioactive cloud from a Ukraine nuclear power plant mentioned earlier, thousands of lives were lost and the government was essentially helpless in stopping the contamination. As set forth below, a similar scenario in a major American metropolitan area, a Three Mile Island–type incident that blows the lid off as it did in Chernobyl, or the rupture of a chemical plant as happened at an American company's facility in India, would cause the death of hundreds of thousands—*and the survivors would have to make it on their own because of the nature and enormity of the disaster.*

Do we really need to plan for a disaster?

Don't terrorist attacks, nuclear power plant meltdowns, and chemical plant or train car explosions happen so infrequently that we will probably spend our entire lives without encountering one?

How realistic is it that we will encounter a need for disaster planning in our lives?

Anyone who isn't aware that we live in a dangerous world has been hiding their heads in the sand—and they better lift their heads and look around or they may find themselves buried in it.

I have experienced two killer earthquakes; been stuck in the heart of a major inner city riot that involved killing, looting, and burning; sought shelter in a storm cellar during a tornado; had friends and relatives evacuated from their homes twice by hurricanes and twice by forest fires; had a nut stick a gun in my gut; been robbed on two continents; and seen my brother and his family have to evacuate from their home when a train carrying munitions began exploding nearby. After I returned from seeing the pyramids in Egypt, dozens of tourists were gunned down at an attraction I had visited only weeks before.

While these scenarios pale in significance to what a pioneer endured on a daily basis, our forefathers were not born into an age in which the worse nightmares of man-made Armageddon, the survival of the human race, might be in the hands of a suicidal terrorist with a suitcase nuke, or where religious fanatics could kill thousands of people by flying airplanes into buildings.

The first major terrorist incident aimed at civilians on American soil, the World Trade Center bombing in New York City in 1993, was a near miss in terms of causing thousands of deaths. It was followed by the murderous Oklahoma City bombing in 1995, and the horrific enormity of the 9/11 tragedy in 2001.

Besides these three major events and the many attacks on Americans and American facilities around the world, potential terrorist attacks in cities ranging from Seattle, San Francisco, and Los Angeles in the West, across the country to the Midwest and South, and all along the East Coast, have been foiled by governmental investigations.

Materials found in terrorist manuals reveal that terrorism has evolved from plots to plant bombs that cause local destruction to grandiose schemes that inflict widespread damage and casualties. The plan was not just to murder innocent people, but to strike a crippling blow that would create confusion and paralyze the government, permitting terrorist cells to move into action.

There are literally thousands of targets in the United States in the form of nuclear reactors and chemical plants scattered from coast to coast and border to border that terrorists can use to satisfy their murderous lust.

How easy is it to learn the survival techniques for this new age of threats to our survival?

Each threat will be dealt with at length. While we will draw heavily on reports and recommendations from governmental disaster agencies, the critical points you need to know will be summarized.

The idea is not to become an expert on survival tactics unless you have the time and desire. If you do, there is enough material included in this book to get you started.

Most of you will only use the basics—you need to know the minimum necessary to give yourself a better chance to stay alive. Trying to learn too much would be self-defeating because you will not remember it.

The most prudent and reasonable course for most of you is to learn the critical tactics for the dangers our security agencies have designated as the most probable to occur.

You will first review the specific dangers you face—surprisingly, one of the hazards you hear about constantly has the least threat to your safety. Following the review, the survival tactics needed for each hazard will be outlined. You will learn that basically the same reaction is used in most scenarios. Then you will go through step-by-step preparations. Detailed instructions from the security agencies will follow the outlines.

A DANGEROUS
WORLD

What dangers do we realistically need to plan for?

Do you recall the story of the biblical Four Horsemen of the Apocalypse? They are the scourges that are predicted to bring war, famine, pandemic disease, and death upon the earth during the last days. There are actually five horsemen in the biblical account, not four. After the white, red, and black horsemen came the fourth horseman, the "pale horsemen whose name was Death." Following Death came a fifth horseman whose name was Hell.

The biblical banes about sum up the dangers we face: They add up to hell.

In more precise terms, the hazards are biological agents, chemical toxins, radiological dust, and nuclear explosions. There is also a hazard from conventional explosives, such as suicidal bombers—ranging from individuals packing explosives strapped to them, to mass murderers at the helm of hijacked jetliners.

CONVENTIONAL EXPLOSIVES

The hazards from explosions themselves are little dealt with in the security agency guides for two reasons: (1) as individuals, other than keeping a sharp eye out for suspicious people and objects, there is little we can do about the threat; and (2) just as the 9/11 terrorists used their flying bombs to make the greatest kills, it is expected that the explosion itself will not cause the greatest damage, but a catastrophic by-product of the initial explosion will—for example, flying a suicide plane into a nuclear reactor, a chemical storage tank, or an occupied high-density building. Thus it's the by-product of an explosion that we have to plan for.

These comments are in no way intended to negate the powerful effect of a conventional explosion itself. We saw a horrendous effect on 9/11, not to mention the effects of homegrown terrorism on the Oklahoma City federal building where nearly two hundred lives were lost from what was essentially a load of fertilizer and farm chemicals.

But terrorists, with their mass-murder mentalities, are expected to attempt to increase their kill ratio, so we need to understand how explosives combined with other hazards dramatically increase the threat to us.

With that in mind, let's look at the Four Horsemen that governmental security agencies hawk the most: biological, chemical, radiological, and nuclear dangers.

BIOLOGICAL AGENTS

Those of us long past high school biology should stop and con-sider what a biological agent is. Anthrax is a good example to review because it was in the news so often after a crazy mailed out doses of it.

Anthrax is a microscopic life-form, a very "tiny animal" (as the Victorians used to refer to microbes). This creature is so small that twenty billion spores of pure Anthrax amount to less than a teaspoon. Even though the existence of anthrax as a danger to humans is new to most of us, it is not new to historians or scientists. It is, in fact, the likely cause of one of the oldest recorded diseases inflicting animals—it is believed by many modern scholars to have been described by Moses in Exodus, and by the classical authors of Greek and Roman antiquity (from Homer and Hippocrates to Virgil and Galen).

Before its characteristics were understood in the nineteenth century, anthrax sometimes spread like a plague. The basic pattern was that humans would become infected by handling the hides or eating the meat of farm animals like cattle and sheep that were already infected. It played a major role in the development of the science of biology—it was the first disease in which a microorganism was definitely demonstrated as the cause, and the first infectious disease in which a bacterial vaccine proved effective (a crude "vaccine" for the smallpox virus developed long before the anthrax bacterial one).

Like many other microscopic biological creatures, anthrax is an aquatic beast—it thrives when it gets into a liquid environment in which it can feed.

Our bloodstreams are a perfect breeding ground for it. The easiest way to get anthrax into the bloodstream is to breathe it into your lungs through your nose or mouth. It can also enter by coming in contact with your eyes or through a cut on your skin. Once it makes the journey into your bloodstream, it quickly begins to multiply—two become four, four become eight, and so on.

Very soon, usually less than a day, there are so many of these creatures in your bloodstream that you are terminal. I have read a statistic that if there wasn't anything to stop these microorganisms from doubling in a short period of time, they would soon be a mass the size of the Earth. Fortunately, there is something to stop them—starvation. If they don't have an unlimited food supply, they can't keep multiplying. They soon kill their human host and hope to be picked up by another host before they die (the anthrax microbe can turn itself into a spore and live for decades while waiting for another host to latch onto).

The most likely way any of us would get infected by anthrax, either from a homegrown or foreign terrorist, or by accident at a lab or in transit, would be by breathing in the organism. And the most likely way of delivering it would be sending an envelope containing a powder with anthrax mixed in, unleashing it through an air-conditioning system, or dropping it from an airplane.

There are many ways anthrax could be spread. Whichever way it is released, it is not likely that it would have the widespread effect of threats such as the rupture of a tank at a chemical plant. One reason is that, unlike with microbes such as ordinary flu and smallpox, anthrax is not contagious (although if someone came into contact with it, it still may be present on the person's body or clothing). It also would be difficult to amass large quantities of it. Unlike chemical and radiological threats, large quantities of anthrax are not being stored. Nevertheless, it is possible for large quantities to be produced and spread over a large group of people, but doing so would take special skills and equipment.

Unlike anthrax, some biological agents, smallpox for example, are very infectious and can spread to epidemic—and pandemic—proportions if precautions are not taken. But, as we know from the spread of other highly infectious diseases like severe acute respiratory syndrome (SARS), infectious diseases can be controlled in countries like the United States and Canada where there is medical knowledge and skilled medical treatment and equipment.

Despite the tragic deaths and tremendous fears generated by anthrax-tainted letters and the real-life horrors of a smallpox infection, biological agents are not the most serious threat facing us. They can kill us as individuals and can be spread over a small area, but they are difficult for an untrained terrorist to produce, handle, and spread. Thus, despite their fear-inspiring nature, biological hazards are unlikely to be the weapon of choice for mass murderers like terrorists. Instead, they likely have more appeal to the technically inclined crazy who has the knowledge to make them or has access to them.

I am sure that most of us can use a little imagination and figure out a way for a terrorist to kill thousands with a biological agent, everything from spraying it over the Super Bowl arena to pouring it into a city's drinking water, but to put it in terms that are brutal but realistic—there are easier ways for the perpetrator to kill us than having to deal with the complexities of bio agents. It may come as a surprise to many people, but an atomic bomb is less complex to handle than a vial of smallpox.

Nothing I have said is intended to diminish the potential killing power of biological agents. Many biological threats are much more lethal than chemical or radiological ones. For example, botulinum, a bacteria which most frequently affects people who eat improperly canned food, is one of the most potent poisons on the planet. It is several million times more potent than sarin, a chemical nerve gas.

CHEMICAL AGENTS

Chemical threats share some characteristics with biological agents—both hazards pollute the air, making it toxic to us, and both can be spread quickly by the wind. However, chemicals constitute a much greater threat to us from a terrorist or even an accidental release than bio agents.

Chemical agents have a history of being spread both intentionally by terrorists in this country and abroad, and of having dire consequences when released by accident or misfortune.

I mentioned the harrowing conclusions of the Environmental Protection Agency (EPA) earlier. That governmental agency, assigned the task of protecting our air, has identified over a hundred chemical plants in the United States where an accidental or deliberate discharge could create a million casualties, and over seven thousand plants that could threaten more than a thousand people. It also discovered that security was lax or nonexistent at most of the plants.

Let's take a look at what this actually means to us as individuals and on the community level. Essentially, whether the ultimate product is for farm use—such as a pesticide, or industrial or home use, such as a solvent—a chemical plant at some stage commonly produces *poison*. When a storage tank full of a toxic chemical is exposed to the air, wind picks up the poison and carries it. There are literally thousands of chemical spills in North America every year, from accidents at plants to accidents involving tanker trucks and railroad tankers.

For example, the 2005 South Carolina new year was ushered in by a rail accident that spread toxic chlorine gas. Nine people were killed and nearly six thousand people evacuated. Had the accident occurred in a major metro area, the casualty rate would have been staggering.

We have yet to experience a major exposure to chemicals that threaten a widespread area—to date, none of the over seven thousand plants have had an accident that has caused deaths into the thousands. But an American plant in India did have such an accident.

Previously referred to as the worst single accidental chemical disaster in history is the deadly gas leak at a Union Carbide (a Connecticut company) plant in India. Poisonous methyl isocyanate gas leaked into the air from a tank at a pesticide plant. The leak was caused by a series of human errors and mechanical problems (both the plant's safety equipment and personnel failed to detect the massive leak for an hour).

Exposed to the air, the chemical formed a large cloud that moved with the wind. The poisonous chemical cloud moved over a densely populated area around midnight. People were in bed, sleeping, when the toxic air invaded their homes. Many people ran into the streets in pain and panic as their eyes and lungs burned from the toxic gas.

It was a nightmare seemingly without end: thousands died quickly, but in the years following the exposure, the casualty list has grown. Some estimates claim that over twenty thousand people have died because of the incident, with another sixty thousand severely disabled, and as many as one million sustaining less mortal injuries.

Tragically, ignorance by the people who let the disaster happen caused the problem, but ignorance on the part of the victims made it worse. Like the enormous disaster in Chernobyl, human error was a major cause, but the lack of knowledge by people who are in the range of danger was also at fault—and with thousands of chemical tanks scattered around the country, almost all of us are in that danger zone. Later in the book, I will review the preparation and survival tactics that could have saved thousands of lives during the Union Carbide chemical leak.

There have also been several intentional acts of "chemical" terrorism that caused deaths, one of which almost succeeded in having as horrendous an effect as 9/11.

We all know that the second World Trade Center murderous attack on 9/11 involved flying commercial jetliners into buildings. The mass murder of innocent people was committed with complex training, planning, and execution (with the technology ranging from box cutters to navigating large passenger jets).

However, the first World Trade Center bombing, eight years earlier in 1993, is a much more typical terrorist attack, a simplified plan of attack that has been used many hundreds of times around the world. It was very nearly a disaster on the scale of 9/11. It deserves our attention because it has so many of the contingencies that we must be aware of, and from the point of view of terrorists, it requires a much lower level of planning and preparation.

The plan for 1993 was simplicity itself: Terrorists constructed a bomb from substances like agricultural fertilizer and other chemicals (somewhat similar in concept to the bomb Timothy McVeigh created for the Oklahoma City bombing).

Driven by a crazed mentality, these fanatics added a poisonous kicker to the concoction: sodium cyanide, which would vaporize in the explosion and send a toxic gas up the air vents and elevator shafts and out onto the streets, killing thousands with the fumes.

They loaded the bomb ingredients, which weighed around thirteen hundred to fourteen hundred pounds, into the back of a rental van and drove it into an underground parking area under Tower One. A macabre aside concerns the van: The size of the bomb was limited by the size of the van—it is claimed that a van was rented rather than a larger truck because the plotters were low on cash. Had they more money, they would have rented a larger truck and purchased more explosives, giving the bombers a better chance to knock down the building. (There's one problem with the truck versus van theory: It's likely with more money they would have rented two vans rather than a larger truck because of the height limitations of underground parking areas.)

It's estimated that the bomb cost no more than about three hundred dollars to construct. It was triggered by an inexpensive fuse lit by a cheap cigarette lighter.

Fortunately, the bomb did not do the widespread damage planned. It knocked a hole about a hundred feet wide through four concrete levels and sent up a cloud of smoke. Six people were killed, hundreds were injured, but the thousands of casualties hoped for by these crazies did not materialize because the buildings did not topple. More important, because these terrorists lacked knowledge in how to construct a poisonous gas bomb, the cyanide poison was burned up by the heat of the explosion.

This type of attack where a bomb explodes in a large building, a subway station during commuter time, or at a crowded sporting event or other public gathering has been the modus operandi of terrorists for decades. They happen around the world on almost a daily basis.

In this country, a homegrown terrorist killed nearly two hundred people with the "fertilizer" bomb that cruelly destroyed the Oklahoma City federal building, while other deaths have occurred from a bomb in Atlanta (not to mention churches, gay bars, and abortion clinic bombings and fires, and biological terrors like anthrax transmitted nationwide by carriers such as the U.S. Postal Service).

One of the strangest incidents of homegrown terrorism occurred in a remote part of the Arizona desert.

The Sunset Limited, an Amtrak train, derailed after bolts

were removed from a joint connecting the rail tracks. A warning system was bypassed with electric wire. The train derailed, killing one person and injuring nearly a hundred more. The train went off the tracks just thirty feet from a bridge—the casualty toll would have been much higher had it gone off the bridge.

The Sons of Gestapo left a note at the train tragedy claiming responsibility and condemning the federal government for their actions at Ruby Ridge and Waco.

None of these attacks has involved attempts to create a deadly chemical cloud other than the first World Trade Center attack, and in that incident the chemicals did not spread over a wide area.

Obviously, these attacks are not just epidemic to America, but have occurred throughout the world, including on an almost daily basis in Israel, Iraq, Afghanistan, and other places in the Middle East.

A deadly chemical attack occurred in 1995 in the Tokyo subway system during rush hour. Twelve people were killed and over five thousand injured when a deadly nerve gas, sarin, was released by Japanese religious fanatics called Aum Shinrikyo, "Supreme Truth." Another chemical attack in a residential area of Tokyo is also attributed to the Japanese terrorists.

The point to all these bombings and suicide attacks is that only one of them, 9/11, involved thousands of deaths, and only a few created a death toll in the hundreds. While even one death or serious injury is a tragedy to the victim and the victim's loved ones, the potential death toll for using conventional explosives to rupture chemical tanks has the potential to create tragedy again on a national level.

As with biological and other hazards, we will return to the subject of chemical dangers when we discuss survival tactics and preparation.

However, it should be noted as we go to the next subject, radiological hazards, that chemical and radiological hazards share a common denominator: They are man-made hazards that pose an incredible danger to us as much from an accidental occurrence as one created deliberately.

RADIOLOGICAL HAZARDS

Radiological in this context refers to the dangers created by "dirty bombs" and nuclear power plants. A third radiological threat, a nuclear bomb, will be discussed elsewhere.

We all know that our bodies get a dose of radiation every day from our natural environment—it's just when the dosage exceeds normal levels that we need to be concerned. If we are caught in the spread of radioactive material from a bomb or nuclear reactor, we can quickly get a deadly dose.

The threat of radioactive exposure is one of the most serious dangers facing us.

A "dirty bomb" is a radioactive device, but it is not an atomic bomb like the ones dropped on Japan during World War II or the warheads of missiles in silos and submarines during the Cold War.

It essentially is a conventional explosive device (the type of explosive used by terrorists to kill people and destroy buildings almost every day on this dangerous planet) linked to a uranium source. A classic example would be to use a high-intensity explosive charge (like the fertilizer-based bombs used at the first

World Trade Center attack and in the Oklahoma City bombing) to spread uranium that has been added to the concoction. A source of the uranium could be fuel that had been used in a nuclear reactor. That source and others have created millions of gallons of radioactive waste being stored in what investigations reveal are facilities that do not have adequate security.

The purpose of a dirty bomb is to increase the kill range of a conventional explosion by fouling the air with poisonous radioactive material and polluting the physical area with a substance that will still be poisonous in hundreds of years.

When the bomb explodes, the initial damage zone depends on its ingredients—but you wouldn't have the nuclear explosion that occurs with an atomic bomb with its characteristic mushroom cloud, massive destruction, and firestorm. Instead, it scatters the radioactive materials over a wide area, preferably into the air, so that the materials are carried in the wind like fine dust—*lethal fine dust*.

There are differences between vaporous or gaseous chemical clouds and radioactive dust, but they both serve the purpose of killing or injuring people who come into contact with them. One difference between a chemical and a radioactive discharge is that the latter is usually infinitely more difficult to clean up. It has often taken decades for high-tech crews to clean up after accidents at nuclear facilities.

From information obtained from investigations, our security agencies believe that a dirty bomb is a weapon of civilian terror and murder now being considered by terrorist groups.

Besides the radioactive waste storage sites in this country, there is a rich supply of dirty bomb uranium from nuclear reactors and waste sites around the world, some of which are in countries like Pakistan and Iran that are breeding grounds for Islamic jihad fundamentalists. Another major source is the widespread black market in used and unused nuclear reactor fuels and bomb-grade uranium that erupted in the wake of the dissolution of the Soviet Union.

Despite popular misconceptions, nuclear-type fuels are relatively easy to handle, much easier than biological agents like anthrax, and generally do not present a high danger of exploding while being handled.

Baby boomers were raised on the notion that uranium would burn holes through you like a laser beam, and that's certainly possible if that is the objective, but the truth is that while uranium is highly toxic and extremely dangerous under some circumstances, much of the time it can be handled with your bare hands.

I wouldn't handle the stuff with *my* bare hands—but I have read scientific information about how easy it is to handle uranium. Having been raised in an era where backyard bomb shelters were more pervasive than swimming pools, however, my rational mind refuses to accept the theory that you can scoop up bomb-grade uranium in your hands—even if you don't have any cuts—and live to tell about it.

The second major radiological danger is many times more dangerous than a dirty bomb. In a way, it is the mother of dirty bombs: your friendly neighborhood nuclear reactor.

In terms of potentially dangerous levels of radiation, the main source of the danger in peacetime are the reactors, which are the core of nuclear power plants that generate electricity (there are also nuclear reactors used in research and other sectors). The word *reactor* means exactly that: rods of uranium are exposed to each other, causing the uranium to react and heat up. The heat is applied to liquids that turn turbines to produce electricity. The process is not unlike how electricity is produced with fossil fuels like coal, oil, and natural gas.

The reason for nuclear reactors is simple: *One pound of uranium yields as much energy as three million pounds of coal.*

But with that efficiency comes a terrible threat: The potential danger to mankind from the uranium used in the reactors and the spent uranium being stored can be measured in centuries, not just our lifetimes.

However, the biggest danger to us is not the theft of uranium from a reactor or waste site. A dirty bomb made by combining

stolen uranium with conventional explosions could cruelly devastate a densely populated area, but it pales in significance *to
turning a nuclear power plant into a bomb.*

Besides Fukushima, to date, there have been three major nuclear power plant "meltdowns" that have been widely documented.
The place in the reactor where nuclear fission occurs is called the
core. In simple terms, the core is the heart of the reactor where the
uranium rods react and heat up. If the reactor operator permits
the rods to overheat, or if overheating happens because of mechanical failure, there is a danger of a meltdown during which
the uranium gets so hot, it goes out of control. If you push the gas
pedal on your car so that the car revs too high, you can stop the
engine by letting up on the pedal and turning it off with the key.
With a nuclear reactor, once it overheats, there is a critical point
at which nothing can stop the meltdown.

Surrounding the reactor is a containment shell of steel, concrete, and other reinforcement materials. When the reactor goes
out of control, a *local explosion* can occur that literally blows
away the containment shell, which means it devastates the reactor
and the immediate surrounding area, as opposed to a massive,
wide-reaching explosion like an atomic bomb.

But even though the explosion itself only damages the immediate area of the reactor, the reactor has the ability to send an
enormous amount of radioactive material (for convenience's sake,
we will call it *radioactive dust*) miles into the sky. As we learned
from Chernobyl, the most devastating nuclear reactor accident
in history, dust can be carried over a huge area, thousands of
square miles, killing and otherwise harming people and animals.

The nuclear reactor at Chernobyl was at a plant that generated electricity. The plant was built by the Soviets in the Ukraine
area during the late 1970s. In 1986, errors in human judgment
combined with mechanical failure permitted the reactor to get
out of control. When the operators lost control and were unable
to shut the reactor down, a meltdown occurred that literally
blew the roof off the place.

The explosion sent radioactive material miles into the atmosphere, where the "dust" was then picked up by wind currents. Because of the difficulty of putting out a fiery uranium meltdown, it took over a week to contain, during which time more tons of radioactive material shot into the air.

The calamity produced several times more radiation than that created by the atomic bombs dropped on Hiroshima and Nagasaki.

Radiation—long-lasting poison—was spread by the wind over a three-nation area. Millions of acres of farmland and forest were contaminated—along with the people living there. The area directly contaminated and rendered dangerous by the contamination was nearly eleven thousand square miles, an area larger than the states of Massachusetts and Rhode Island put together. Elevated radiation levels were reported as far away as France.

While only the people working at the plant were instantly killed by the Chernobyl explosion, the death toll over the past couple of decades is in the tens of thousands and will probably soar to the hundreds of thousands due to the long-term cancer risk of exposure to radiation. The fact that the Soviet government actively tried to cover up the incident makes health statistics difficult to obtain—but the ones we know are horrifying.

There have also been two near-miss accidents in which reactors got out of control and nearly caused catastrophic damage and loss of life.

The first occurred in northwest England in the late 1950s. The Windscale nuclear reactor facility and plutonium production plant in the Cumberland area went out of control during a routine heating operation. The overheating caused uranium cartridges to rupture, resulting in a release of radioactivity and a fire that burned for sixteen hours before it was extinguished (ten tons of radioactive fuel were left in the melted core after the fire).

The smoke and dust sent up by the fire also caused the release of a considerable amount of radioactive iodine into the air. The British government tried to minimize the seriousness of the situation—but banned the sale of milk in a two-hundred-square-mile area. The reactor area was sealed and a cleanup began about thirty years later, in the late 1980s.

The second incident was Three Mile Island. This nuclear power plant is located at the Susquehanna River near Harrisburg, Pennsylvania. In 1979, about four in the morning, mechanical failure, human error, and bad decisions during the next few hours resulted in the loss of water coolant to the reactor core. The reactor was shut down by its safety system, but as a result of human mistake, the emergency system was shut off and major core damage occurred, allowing radioactive material to escape. Even though decades have passed, part of the reactor is still unusable.

Through good fortune, the danger to the public was minimal according to the Nuclear Regulatory Commission (NRC).

When you realize the scope of the Chernobyl disaster, and then compare that to the information on nuclear plant dangers given out by the NRC, you have to wonder how much of the nuclear power industry lobbyists' money went into the campaign chests of our members of Congress.

Despite the lessons learned from Chernobyl, the NRC simply does not give out convincing advice on the dangers of nuclear power plants. Apparently, the agency's loyalty to the big companies who own the plants is greater than its loyalty to the people who are threatened by the malfunction of one.

A big lie concerns its emergency planning zones that limit the direct radiation threat to humans to a ten-mile radius of the plant (a ten-mile radius comprises a circle five miles in each direction from the plant).

The NRC also states that radioactive materials could contaminate water supplies, food crops, and livestock within up to a fifty-mile radius (which translates to twenty-five miles in each direction from the plant).

I have no doubt that the statements made by the NRC are completely true. The statements are not lies by express misrepresentations, but *lies by omissions*. Clever wording hides the truth.

For example, the zone that threatens humans has been unreasonably limited to near the plant by the clever way the assessment is worded. But you don't have to be a rocket scientist to find a credibility gap as deep as the Grand Canyon in the advisement: In the minds of these bureaucrats, the fact that food, water, and animals will be poisoned for twenty-five miles in every direction, or fifty miles if the wind is blowing right, is not a hazard to people in the area.

Do the bureaucrats at the NRC think the air we breathe is different from the air the dogs, cats, and horses in the neighborhood breathe? Are they under the impression that even if food, water, and animals are threatened, humans are not going to be affected? And those "direct" effects do not have to be immediate death from radiation burns. Aren't you "directly" harmed if you breathe, drink, or eat radiation that in future years will lead to death from cancer?

To water down the threat from a nuclear plant when there is no model to evaluate the threat with is only slightly criminal. But it's aiding and abetting mass murder to make such a statement when we have the example of Chernobyl.

Not everything about nuclear power plants is bad. They do produce electricity cheaper and cleaner than power plants that use fossil fuels. The problem is that in today's world of human error and mass murderers wearing the masks of terrorists, they present an unacceptable danger to all of us.

By the way—because the potential damage that can be caused by a nuclear power plant is so great, *they cannot be insured for catastrophic damages*. Congress passed a special law exempting them from having to be insured for major disasters.

Now that's a comforting thought. . . .

Bottom line: Nuclear power plants are here to stay, regardless of how dangerous they are. That does not make them good neighbors, especially in this age of terrorism. But they are here, so our goals should be to make them safe, sane, and protected from terrorists.

As terribly tragic as the 9/11 plane crash in Pennsylvania was

to those on board and their loved ones, the scope of the 9/11 tragedy would have been astronomically higher if that plane had hit
the nuclear power plant at Three Mile Island, which is near Harrisburg, Pennsylvania.

Philadelphia, with a metro base of over six million people, is
only about a hundred miles away.

10

NUCLEAR TERRORISM

Nuclear devices, essentially atomic bombs or nuclear weapons, are more familiar to us than the concept of dirty bombs and exploding nuclear reactors. We have a history of atomic warfare—two atomic bombs were exploded against Japan (in Hiroshima and Nagasaki during World War II), causing upwards of a couple hundred thousand deaths.

What is not familiar to us is the ease with which today's terrorists can obtain nuclear devices. We already spoke of the collapse of the Soviet Union and the breakdown of finances and authority that left that nation's nuclear facilities hemorrhaging weapons of mass destruction—there have been hundreds of incidences of bomb-grade uranium being sold on the black market and reports that dozens of suitcase nukes are missing.

What is a suitcase nuke? As explained earlier in the book, it's a small nuclear device, an atomic bomb that can be carried to a detonation site by car. Dozens of suitcase nukes disappeared from the Soviet nuclear stockpiles after the fall of the Soviet Union.

Regardless of the availability of the suitcase nukes, the fact is that an atomic bomb can be assembled from instructions obtained on the Internet—and the materials appear to be available in the former Soviet states literally at yard sales. It does not take high-tech equipment to explode one—atomic bomb technology is less complex than flying and navigating a big passenger jet.

This book is not the place to discuss the incredibly real threat of nuclear terrorism, a threat of apocalyptic proportions, but we need to acknowledge that the threat exists—that is the warning from our federal security agencies.

The most immediate and deadly effect of a nuclear device is the explosion and fire, annihilating everyone in the device's kill range. The immediate danger to anyone far enough away to survive the fiery devastation is deadly air. Like a dirty bomb, a nuclear device creates radioactive dust that can be carried for miles.

While the dirty bomb and exploding nuclear reactor do not create as much initial damage as a nuclear device, the consequences for people far enough away to use survival tactics are basically the same for each danger.

11

SURVIVAL TACTICS

The FEMA guide included in this book is very valuable because it contains a wealth of information—but as one would expect from the government, it does err on the side of giving too much information. This is especially true when it comes to the preparation and tactics needed to survive the main dangers (biological agents, chemical fumes, radiological dust, and nuclear devices).

From the viewpoint of governmental emergency planners and emergency workers, it is necessary to understand all the different complications of the various threats—obviously, a biological agent like anthrax mixed with powder has to be handled differently than radioactive dust. But the person facing the hazard is not in the same shoes as a professional rescue worker who has the training and equipment to deal with the problem.

The categorical imperative of the person swept up in the dangerous maelstrom of a terrorist's dirty bomb or catastrophic accidental discharge at a nuclear power plant is simply to *survive*.

Survival first depends upon *where you are when danger strikes*. Obviously, there are different "zones" in a disaster area:

There is the *kill zone,* in which people are killed, mortally wounded, or injured so badly that they cannot fend for themselves and can only hope for rescue.

Then there is the *escape zone*—you have missed being killed or rendered helpless by the initial incident and now you have a chance to survive, *but you need to do something.* You may or may not be injured, but you are still mobile or otherwise able to take some action to save your life and those of your loved ones.

By referring to the area as the escape zone, I am not implying that the best reaction in all circumstances is to attempt to flee the danger. As we will see from the survival tactics set out in the next chapter, running is sometimes the worst possible alternative. The word *escape* is being used here simply to connote that we have to do something *fast.*

PREPARATION, PREPARATION, PREPARATION

Our chances of survival soar if we have prepared ourselves mentally for the escape zone. Getting people prepared is the goal of this book and the objective of the copious information provided by our federal security agencies.

Mental preparation is similar to sports training. If you have played a fast-moving sport—tennis, basketball, table tennis, etc.—you know that your mind and body have to be trained so that your muscles move without conscious thought because the action is often too fast for you to think about what your next move should be.

That is what preparation is all about—knowing what to do without giving it much thought.

12

THE ESCAPE ZONE

I mentioned earlier that the people actually facing a danger have different contingencies they must deal with than professional rescue workers. Not only do the rescue workers have training and equipment, they also often have better information about what they are facing.

In the minutes (or longer, depending on the circumstances) that it takes rescue workers to go into action, there is an opportunity to realize what the threat is—and even when they do not know the exact nature of the threat, they may have the equipment to defend themselves from a number of different dangers.

The contingencies facing ordinary people in a crisis are different. A realistic picture of what happens is this:

First, there is the violent incident. Let's say it's an explosion, since that is the basis for most terrorist and accidental incidences. From the explosion may come smoke, dust, debris, and fire.

What do you do?

If there is fire or another known hazard such as falling debris, you must get to safety. You don't need a book or a complex guide to tell you that. The rest of this discussion assumes that you have survived the initial devastation and that you are not in immediate danger of fire or falling objects.

At this point, we will assume that you are in the escape zone— *which is the assumption you should make*. Why? Because you don't know if there is a secondary hazard. The 9/11 attack created a secondary hazard after the initial impact by the enormous buildings crashing down. The 1993 World Trade Center attack included a secondary hazard of a poisonous chemical attack that was intended to kill thousands. Homeland Security has repeatedly warned that the agency expects airborne hazards following an initial attack.

Unless there is the telltale mushroom of an atomic bomb, you are not going to know what danger you are facing. But you do know one extremely vital fact: Regardless of the nature of the danger, whether the hazard is biological, chemical, radiological, or even nuclear, *your primary enemy will be poisonous air*.

Again, this assumes you have survived the initial explosion/ fire/debris and are still on your feet. But to hit the point again: There is nothing you can do about those dangers except hope you are still alive and mobile. Being prepared for fire and explosion is limited to knowing escape routes from the place you are in. By now, I am assuming that your survival instinct is well honed enough so that you do not need another lecture about taking a moment to find the exits wherever you are.

The simple fact that toxic air is the main threat to civilians is not emphasized by the security agencies charged with our protection. But again, bad air is the hazard because:

- As an individual, you cannot realistically do anything about the explosion/fire/falling debris.
- In the immediate moments following the disaster, it will be unlikely that you will know what further dangers you face— whether there is a biological, chemical, or radiological agent in the air.

- As we learned from 9/11, there are tremendous poisonous air dangers even when there is no planned biological, chemical, or radiological agent included.

Whether you are at work, at school, in your home, in a vehicle, or on the street, the reaction to each of those situations is the same: *protect your breathing*.

If you are out in the open, the first instinct you will likely have is to run (flee on foot or by vehicle)—to put as much distance between you and the initial explosion as possible. Unless you see a cloud of hazardous substance, you probably are in complete ignorance as to what further danger exists. But you do know that the danger will likely be in the form of something you breathe through your mouth or nose (or take in through your eyes, cuts, and/or bare skin).

Let's say you have survived the initial explosion and are not immediately threatened by fire or debris, but you know that there could be a bio/chemical or radiological hazard in the air. At this point you have a choice: *Do you run or hide?*

The conventional wisdom is not to run! You should seek shelter.

Why? Because you don't know what you are running from or which direction to run. In other words, you may jump out of the frying pan and into the fire.

Not to run is easier said than done. Since you won't know the exact danger you are facing, it comes down to an individual choice as to what action to take—with as much science behind the choice as deciding by the flip of a coin.

If you are at home and a toxic cloud comes your way, your best chance of survival is probably in a safe room. This concept is discussed at length later, but essentially it is a small room (such as a bathroom) with as few windows as possible where you can retreat to and then seal off with whatever is handy.

Once in the room, you should do everything you can to protect your breathing.

Hopefully, you have already prepared a basic safe room kit. The kits are discussed at length later but they are basically plastic sheets, tape, and N95 dust masks available at your local hardware store. Turn off any incoming air/heat vents and seal the vents.

Escape hoods for people who work in high-rise buildings are also discussed in a separate section, but essentially they are a head covering similar to the hood of a coat, with a clear plastic face (so you can see) and a filtered breathing apparatus. Escape hoods are also called smoke hoods. Their purpose is to keep your eyes and breathing clear long enough for you to get out of a building where there is fire smoke or another airborne hazard.

If you don't have a safe room, or if you are caught somewhere besides home—at work, in a hotel, on the street—the procedure is the same: Get into a room with as few openings as possible, and seal the openings (use your clothes to seal cracks of doors if necessary) and air vents.

Keep in mind that if you are on the street, you should not try to outrun an airborne hazard by foot if there is any type of shelter available. Get into a building (or a parked vehicle if that is all that's available). Getting out of the open and having solid walls between you and the hazard is critical. Protect your breathing (and eyes) as much as possible with clothing. A poisonous gas will find its way through tiny openings, but you can reduce the risk by getting as many walls between you and the hazard as you can.

Some chemical poisons and radioactive dust are slightly heavier than air. They flow with the wind and will soon drop. Thus, going higher up in a building helps to avoid some hazards. Getting into a basement or cellar can be better if the area is sealed or sealable. But the problem with the advice of going up or down is that you probably won't know what type of hazard it is, and your first instinct should be to seal off a small room rather than running up the stairs or getting into an elevator that may strand you in an elevator shaft.

If you get in your car to race away, you are gambling that you will outrun it. And you had better have your wits about you to roll up the windows and shut off the air ducts (some cars have air ducts that do not shut off). Even at that, your car will not be sealed.

If I had a choice between trying to seal off a room if I'm at home (or a hotel, an office, the mall, the street) and fleeing in my car . . . unless I had some knowledge of what the hazard was, my personal choice would be to get walls between me and the hazard and seal it as best I can. By the same token, if I was already in a car, it is doubtful I would leave it to find safety from an airborne threat unless I felt that (1) I couldn't outrun it, and (2) I wasn't going to inhale it getting out of the car and going into a building. A parked car with the windows up may not have a tight seal, but it is many steps above being outside with no protection.

What this all comes down to is the simple procedure that has been repeated above but needs to become second nature in your mind: For those of you fortunate to survive fire and explosion, the main threat is air poisoned by windborne biological, chemical, or radiological hazards.

The first reaction has to be to instantly protect your breathing (and your eyes) as much as possible with what you are wearing—*but without delay in getting shelter.* Don't stop and take the time to try and protect your breathing with a handkerchief or what you are wearing. If you can briefly protect your breathing with your hand or a cloth you're wearing, that is good, because even a little protection helps against many hazards (some bio hazards and radioactive dust, for example). But it would not help against many chemical hazards—such as a gaseous substance like nerve gas.

Only attempt to protect your breathing while your feet are moving you as fast as possible into a building or other locale that will put solid walls between you and the hazards. Most of us would instinctively attempt to protect our breathing with something we are wearing, but again, don't do it at the expense of losing precious seconds getting shelter and sealing the shelter as much as possible.

Getting shelter normally is a sounder bet than trying to outrun the hazard because you have little chance of knowing what you are running from, how fast it's coming, or which way it will go.

13

THE SAFE ROOM

A safe room is a place to take shelter during an emergency in which a biological, chemical, or radiological airborne hazard endangers you. It is usually a room you have designated in your own residence (house or apartment), but it can also be a room at work or school.

Remember that old phrase about "my home is my castle"? In most man-made disasters carrying an airborne threat (biological, chemical, radiological, nuclear), it is probably the best place for you.

The idea behind a safe room is to designate a room that has few or no windows and is small enough to seal. It should be a room that fits your needs in terms of the number of people to shelter and how your residence is laid out. Some people choose a bathroom—they are convenient for obvious reasons—and they are often small rooms with no more than one window. A walk-in closet might be a safe room for a single person in a small apartment, but bear in mind that you still need air to breathe after you seal it. If you seal a room with plastic, at some point you will run out of air, so choose a space large enough to have several hours of air after it is sealed.

The safe room in my own house is a bathroom with one door and a single small window. The safe room you designate will depend upon the physical layout of where you live, the number of people you need to shelter, and the type of hazards you live closest to.

Designate a room in the house as the safe room. Discuss with your family why the room was chosen and how it will be used. If there are children involved, rehearse using the room—remember, they may be home alone when the room is needed.

If the room has cracks (such as the opening around plumbing fixtures in a bathroom), use molding clay to close them. There is also a type of nonhardening claylike plumber's putty you can use.

Note each place where poisonous fumes could enter—usually the door(s), window(s), and vent(s).

Once you designate the safe room, you need to "furnish" it. This can be done at an amazingly low price. The recommended items are:

rolls of plastic sheeting—the type you find in paint supply stores

rolls of duct tape—that gray stuff that seems to stick to anything

scissors

an N95 dust mask for each person (see the section on these inexpensive masks that might save your life)

a battery-powered radio

These items take up little space. Store them in the safe room so that they will be there when you need them.

Plastic sheets come in different sizes of thickness; it's not expensive, so don't buy cheap stuff. It's used with the tape to seal the windows, doors, air vents, and other openings.

Don't use the above items prior to an actual emergency. When you realize there is an airborne hazard, retreat into the safe room, immediately close the windows, doors, and vents and seal them.

If you have time and can remember, turn off the air and/or heat system if it pulls air from the outside and distributes it throughout the house—which most systems do.

Should your safe room be in the cellar or toward the attic? It depends upon the hazards you believe you will face. As I mentioned, many chemicals and radiological dust are heavier than air, and thus will eventually fall to the earth, making it safer to be higher up—while higher up is the worst place to be for high winds and tornadoes.

A safe room is not intended for long-term occupancy. Depending on how big the room is, how well sealed it is, how many people are in it, etc., you could run out of breathable air in a relatively short time. Hopefully, a hazard like a chemical cloud or radiation dust would dissipate before you need to leave the room. The purpose of the safe room is to breathe clean air long enough for the initial danger to pass.

If people in the cities near the Union Carbide insecticide plant in India and the Chernobyl nuclear reactor catastrophe had used safe rooms, the casualties suffered would have been a small fraction of those that occurred.

For people who have deep pockets and boundless paranoia, the room actress Jodie Foster retreated into when her home was invaded by robbers in the movie *Panic Room* would make a terrific safe room. I am being facetious, but I am sure there is more than one dot-com billionaire with a panic room engineered by the likes of NASA.

Because most people spend more time in their homes than anywhere else, there is a good chance that is where you will be when danger strikes.

I like to think of the safe room as the castle keep, the place where the last defense of the castle is made. Don't leave it unless you are forced to or are instructed by rescue workers to do so.

If you are forced to leave your safe room and have to go outside, get as much protection to your face as possible (N95 masks and/or clothing) and get into a vehicle if one is available (closing windows and vents). If you know where the danger is coming from, try to move upwind or crosswind from it—moving downwind will keep the hounds of hell on your heels.

Emergency Survival Supplies

The government's recommendation that you have two separate stockpiles of food and water—one for three days and one for two weeks—is not as impractical as it sounds. It is also extremely good advice, regardless of whether you are running from a hurricane or a terrorist threat.

Many people in Florida have what they call "hurricane money" that they can grab and run with.

Think of the emergency supplies as your "survival money." And keep in mind that some things are more important than others.

WATER

Water is more important than food.

Other than people with special dietary needs (children and pregnant women, for example), most of us can go many days without food. We may not like it, but we can do it.

Water is a different matter. We need liquid to avoid dehydration regardless of the weather conditions. We need less liquid in cold than warm climates, but we still need liquid. The time period we can go without water is much shorter than the length of time we can go without food.

There are cases where people have managed to go without food and water for long periods of time—the survive-the-savage-sea-type tales where people have subsisted for weeks or even months, drinking fish blood and their own urine (I have read that drinking your own urine is counterproductive to survival, but there are people who believe it helped them survive).

Thus the three-day and two-week supply should include water and some food items packed in liquid. Whether you live in the desert or the mountains can affect how much water you pack, but a rule of thumb is to have at least two quarts per person per day. That equals out to a total of six gallons for a family of four for three days.

In selecting food items for emergencies, avoid salty food because it increases your need for water.

Some authorities also advise avoiding high-protein foods because protein increases the need for liquid—but protein also packs energy, so you need to be selective about what you omit. (I included a small pack of beef jerky in my three-day kit. It is a completely irrational decision, since jerky is very salty. However, salted beef and hard tack [stone-hard, often saltless biscuits] were the staples of cowboys and pioneers, so I threw in a pack of jerky and a pack of hard crackers for sentimental reasons.)

In terms of sheltering at home, you should store sufficient water for the two-week period. However, you are in a better position at home in terms of water than on the road or sheltering in a strange locale.

There are sources of water in your home you may not instantly think of. If the water in your hot water tank has not been contaminated, you can drain water from the tank through the bottom outlet provided on most tanks. (Note that in the FEMA *Are You Ready?* manual, it states that water used in home heating systems, such as hot water boilers, may not be usable.)

If there is time to pull uncontaminated water into the house, you could fill a bathtub or other containers, but if you do not know at what point contamination occurred this probably is not a good choice. Melted ice cubes are a small source.

Water from many sources should be treated. There are various treatment procedures outlined in the government's manuals for some hazards. Distilling is good for most things except chemical pollution, while other treatments are more limited. A few drops of unscented pure household chlorine bleach helps purify water. The FEMA manual on page 107 of this book describes a simple method of distilling on the stovetop, using a pot, a lid, and a cup.

There are so many different types of hazards and different types of water treatment, you have to determine what the contamination is and what remedy you can use.

If you believe water is essentially clean but want to be a little cautious, try the distilling method (which is the best) and/or bleach. But if you think the water is contaminated, your best bet is to do without water as long as possible because none of the home remedies like boiling, distilling, and adding bleach will clean all types of contamination. (Distilling gets rid of most of them—but not all, especially not chemical contamination.)

Your grab-and-go pack and shelter-at-home supply should both include a small bottle of liquid household-type chlorine bleach (4 to 6 percent sodium hypochlorite) that contains no soap or scents. A small amount of this placed in water (sixteen drops per gallon, left standing for thirty minutes) will kill microorganisms such as bacteria (but not parasites). This chlorine bleach is on most governmental survival lists. Check the FEMA materials (page 107, et seq, of this book) for exact details on treating water. Chlorine itself is toxic, so make sure you use the correct dosage. I used chlorine to purify water while traveling in Mexico for a couple of months when our motorhome purifier went out. But as stated above, chlorine is a harsh, toxic chemical so you have to be careful with it and know exactly how to use it.

The FEMA *Are You Ready?* guidebook has a good discussion about water needs and treatment in general.

FOOD

The three-day supply of food is for grab-and-go emergency purposes—it's for when you're on the run, getting out of harm's way, it's thrown in your car and used en route or while sheltering outside your residence.

The two-week supply of food is for use at home, when you are sheltering inside your residence, while waiting for things to return to normal.

It is not expensive or complicated to come up with an emergency supply of food. Your initial investment is a few hundred dollars and it is essentially a one-time investment—though you should rotate your stock about every six months (even though many commercially canned foods last years), you will be replacing the emergency supply at no extra cost because you make use of the items in your household.

Because you will periodically use the items as nonemergency meals to keep your emergency stock fresh, select emergency items that you will enjoy eating. Keep in mind that advice comes with a couple important caveats.

First, don't confuse *emergency* food with *everyday* food. If you are the type of person who prefers eating the latest dietary fad of "healthy" meals—low carb, low fat, low calorie—or are simply someone who prefers to eat healthy meals that keep you slim, do some rethinking in terms of your three-day grab-and-go survival pack.

You are not stocking food for a lifetime, merely for a few days to eat on the run or at a place of shelter other than your home. You want foods that are high in energy, that pack a lot of nutritional power. You may not have to survive on whale blubber in the arctic, but keep in mind that if you are starving, whale blubber provides more nutrition than rice cakes (I am sure this statement will raise the hackles on the necks of nutritionists, but for emergency food, I believe you want an Eskimo's diet, not that of a fashion model).

Again, the three-day supply is a short-term emergency supply. You are not storing away food for Armageddon. Many people do practice long-term storage. If you are one of them, that's fine, but you still need a three-day grab-and-go supply in case you have to get in your car and head for a shelter or outrun the devil.

The wonderful thing about canned goods is that they are often inexpensive, last a long time, often years, don't have to be cooked, come in containers little affected by temperature and pollution, and are compact. In the "old days," many foods could be heated in the can they were packed in, but I believe the materials currently used will not hold up to heat or will even break down and contaminate food.

All perishable items, including water and canned food, should be dated.

Another consideration is that you should select foods that occupy as little space as possible. For example, peanut butter is a high-energy food that takes up little space in a bag. You will find it on many governmental survival lists (even though many schools won't permit our children to carry peanut butter sandwiches into the lunch room because of possible allergy problems).

On the other hand, rice cakes are wonderful for dieting—but look at this comparison: A package of rice cakes has about *six hundred calories* (units of energy producing values in food). Two jars of peanut butter that would occupy about the same physical space as the package of rice cakes (but weigh more) have a total of over *eight thousand calories*. (The peanut butter also has over twenty times as much protein.)

Going a step further, should you pack rice cakes to smear your peanut butter on? I wouldn't. If you need to spread it on something, find cracker-type items that take up little room and pack more energy.

The second caveat is the space problem. Save treats like potato chips for picnics and rice cakes for dieting; they have little nutritional value and take up too much space. Read labels and pick items that get you the most nutrition per pound. High-energy bars take up little space, so I suppose one could have a three-day supply of just those, but that would become awfully monotonous—and you have to wonder about the nutritional claims on some of them.

Convenience is another factor. Obviously, you need to select items that *do not* have to be cooked. That's the problem with an otherwise terrific portable food source—freeze-dried camping meals. Most of these camping meals need to be cooked in boiling water. Most canned foods do not require cooking—that is why you will see that my own survival pack includes items like canned meats, fish, and beans.

In terms of convenience, easy-to-handle food containers are also useful. A manual can opener is on the list, but I try to find items that don't need a can opener—for example, some fish and meats come in easy-open cans and there are even more convenient foil packages for tuna, salmon, and other items.

The important point is to have it ready, so that all you have to do is throw the bag in the car and be on your way.

There are different types of bags you can use. Some people prefer plastic containers with lids (making them water resistant) but I find the containers stiff and awkward. And they are more difficult to carry than a soft container.

In my mind, a grab-and-go bag is exactly that—a bag. Mine is an old army duffel bag. A military-type, tubular bag is hardy, easy to handle, easy to pack, and can be thrown over your shoulder. Some even have a rubber coating to make them water resistant. You can find these bags in sporting goods stores and army-navy surplus outlets.

Some people might want to invest in a large backpack in case they do have to carry the items some distance. I don't consider the weight of my three-day bag as a significant issue because I don't expect to be carrying the pack long distances. If I have to outrun a hazard on foot, I will be in serious trouble and food will not help me.

Large plastic containers with lids are good for storing your shelter-at-home, two-week food supply because they can be water-, mice-, and insect-resistant. They tend to be cheap and come in many sizes at discount merchandise stores.

To briefly summarize survival food characteristics, choose foods that:

do not need to be cooked

are not perishable over the short term

will not be affected adversely by outside temperature and other weather conditions such as cold, wet, damp, or dry and hot conditions

are high in energy and nutrition, but are compact in size

are packaged so as to avoid contamination from chemical, radiological, etc. pollutants

have some liquid content to help reduce your need for other liquids

are not overly salty (salt increases the need for water)

Note: If you need milk, check out powdered and canned varieties.

MEALS IN A CAN?

The FEMA guide gives good advice about preparing a three-day, grab-and-go bag. I have summarized much of that advice and added my own experiences and ideas to it, but now I want to take the concept a step further.

Again, well-balanced meals are not the objective of the three-day supply. High-energy foods that are easy to handle are the goal. You will either be eating them in a vehicle or in a building you are using for shelter—and neither place is likely to have many amenities. Your best bet is to assume that you will have no table, chairs, stove, etc., and have to deal with the food you have packed.

Getting really practical, and with the knowledge that we can survive on about anything if it's only for three days, and that we have to deal with the limitations of eating and sleeping in a car (which I have done probably a couple hundred times), what sort of food should we realistically pack?

First, forget the balanced meal concept. Second, forget anything that has to be cooked or is perishable. Third, focus on things you will not get sick of if they are eaten repeatedly.

I can't tell you what to select because your tastes will be different from mine. But give thought to a meal that can be provided from the contents of a single, easy-to-open can.

For "meals in a can," check out the large cans of hearty-meal soups with chunks of chicken or beef and vegetables. These cans are a meal in themselves, large enough for most adults. They often come with pop-tops, making them handier to deal with than cans needing a manual opener. Add a pop-top can of fruit and you have dinner in cans that can be eaten in a moving vehicle (except for the driver, of course).

Soups, beans, and other canned foods obviously taste better heated, but you should select foods that are precooked, so they can be eaten without heating.

Some people prefer to purchase MREs (the military-type ready-to-eat meals discussed earlier). You can find a variety of these on the Internet and in survival stores.

Other people prefer high-energy bars that can pack all the energy needed in a single unwrapping.

Bottom line, worrying about a "balanced" meal on the run that takes multiple cans of meat, starch, vegetables, and fruit is too much unnecessary hassle.

PREPACKAGED SURVIVAL FOODS

The Internet and survivalist stores sell emergency rations. I don't know what these things taste like, but they could not be worse than the old army field rations.

MREs (meals ready to eat) are the modern army field rations.

They contain ready-to-eat meals in the twelve-hundred- to fourteen-hundred-calorie range. My understanding is that actual military-issued MREs are illegal to sell, so be careful what you buy—you may not be able to tell how old they are or from what source they came. But there are ready-to-eat meals provided by private companies. MREs and meals in a single bar take up less space, weigh less, and are designed to provide more nutrition than conventional foods.

Because many people cannot afford prepackaged survival foods or prefer foods that satisfy their own tastes, I have included my ideas for food in the list of items for a sample grab-and-go bag.

SAMPLE THREE-DAY GRAB-AND-GO BAG ITEMS

_____ Water: at least a gallon for each person, more if you live in a hot, dry climate or have special needs.

_____ Small plastic bottle of liquid bleach to purify drinking water. Tape specific instructions copied from FEMA to the bottle so you don't use the wrong dosage. You can also use other recommended water purification materials.

_____ Plastic jars of unsalted peanut butter. (Plastic jars are lighter and less fragile than glass—I prefer them over glass for all food items.)

_____ Canned fish in oil. Water-packed is healthier, but not as energy-producing in an emergency. Also check out foil packaging.

_____ Canned meat. Meat with fat is a good emergency food, but note that fat can be hard to eat unless heated.

_____ Canned beans—whatever type you prefer, packed solid or in liquid. Beans are a terrific energy source.

_____ Other canned foods such as soups, vegetables, pastas, rice, and fruit.

_____ Crackers—hard, long lasting, double-sealed in water-proof high-quality freezer bags (these are not as necessary as canned food, but try to eat peanut butter or sardines without them!).

_____ Bags of trail mix containing nuts and dried fruit. Leave them in unopened original containers, then double-seal them in freezer-type plastic bags.

_____ High-energy bars. Check the ingredients carefully to make sure they are what they say they are. Consider a trip to a health food store to check out their supply.

_____ Paper bowls and plastic utensils. Why paper over reusable plastic? Because plastic has to be washed and several dozen paper picnic-type bowls literally fit in the palm of your hand. Bowls are more versatile than flat plates.

_____ Can/bottle opener.

_____ Flashlight. I prefer the four-battery type used by police officers. It can be used for light . . . and for self-defense. A pack of extra batteries would also be useful. I also have a hand-crank flashlight. It is tiring to use for any length of time, but comes in handy because no batteries are needed.

_____ Multipurpose tool that also has Swiss army knife-type blades.

_____ Metal pot that can be used to boil water if necessary.

_____ Warm blankets kept clean in a trash bag in the trunk of the car. It is amazing how many people who live in cold climates freeze to death each year when their cars get stuck in blizzards. I have emergency thermal blankets. The blankets, available over the Internet and in sporting goods stores, are cheap and very small in their packagings, some no bigger than a pack of cigarettes.

_____ A small first-aid kit—with some bandages, something for cuts and scratches, and aspirin (or other pain medication).

_____ Trash bags—for ordinary purposes and possible portable toilets.

_____ Photocopy of critical medical and eye prescriptions. You won't be able to fill your prescriptions en route, but the prescriptions will be handy if you need emergency medical care.

_____ Phone list of friends, relatives, and other significant people.

_____ Radio. This can be crank or battery-operated. NOAA radios (which broadcast everything from weather warnings to Amber Alerts to chemical and nuclear reactor disasters) can also be used. There are portable radios available that have AM/FM as well as weather and audio TV bands. See Emergency Electronics (Chapter 18).

_____ Money in small bills in a waterproof pouch. How much? Not so much that you will be hurting if someone other than yourself grabs it and goes . . . in this age of "plastic," a few hundred dollars might suffice.

_____ A national and regional map. Don't assume that the freeway you know like the back of your hand will be open. And don't assume you can rely upon your GPS (global positioning system)! Keep in mind that paper maps don't need signals from satellites or a power source.

_____ Cigarette lighter(s), the cheap, disposable type. To start a fire with in case one is needed.

_____ Cell phone charger that operates off a car battery (this should be kept in the car at all times anyway).

_____ Compass. To know what direction to go if there are radio broadcasts informing you where a hazard is heading. Again, don't rely upon your GPS alone.

_____ N95 breathing masks. These are important, low-cost items. See the chapter Protective Masks for detailed information. Do include these with your grab-and-go and your shelter-in-place supplies.

_____ Roll of plastic and duct tape. While these are ordinarily used to seal a safe room, you may need them to help seal your car or even a place of temporary shelter. Some people will want to combine their grab-and-go bags with their safe room supplies.

_____ Survival candles—long-burning candles available from Internet sites. Keep in mind that a candle used in a closed area (such as a car or sealed room) quickly burns up the available oxygen.

_____ Checklist. This is one of the most important items to keep in your grab-and-go bag—an itemized list of things you will want to grab _if you have the time_. These are items that are not ordinarily kept in the grab-and-go bag. Some examples are:

    _____ Cell phone and electric charger. Even better than just your cell phone charger is an adapter that plugs into the battery connection of your car (where the cigarette lighter used to be) to charge many different devices.

    _____ Prescription medicines.

    _____ Extra glasses and contact lenses, fluid/container.

_____ Wallet/purse with credit cards, ATM cards, and cash.

_____ Liquid courage (I am being a little facetious, but if movie cowboys are to be believed, brandy, whiskey, and other rotgut come in handy for "medicinal purposes"—snake bites, toothaches, and six-shooter wounds).

_____ A copy of this book.

15

VEHICLE
SURVIVAL KIT

There are times when your vehicle could be your best survival tool. Don't defeat its purpose by failing to keep basic supplies and at least a half tank of gas in it at all times.

The half tank of gas warning arose during the Cold War with the threat of atomic warfare. With today's dangers of radiological and chemical hazards that can affect enormous areas, the advice is being given again.

There are endless stories of people in the Gulf states running out of gas during storm evacuations. As I mentioned above, my brother once got caught with an empty gas tank when a train carrying boxcars loaded with military munitions started exploding near his home.

The list below includes both things that everyone has in their car from the factory (such as the spare and jack) and items that most of would never think of (such as thermal blankets folded no bigger than the size of a pack of cigarettes).

A word about tire jacks—know how to use one before you get caught in the dark and suddenly need the skill. Make sure everyone in the family who is a potential driver knows how to use the jack. Jacks have come a long way from the old bumper jacks that were simple to use (incurring broken bones when used incorrectly). Jacks today can be very complicated. My SUV takes someone akin to the proverbial rocket scientist to figure out how to change one of its tires.

Where you store things will depend on your vehicle. But do not store anything under the driver's seat or the backseat that can make its way to the driver's area. Terrible accidents have occurred because objects have slipped under the brake pedal. In that regard, sadly, most people forget there is an emergency brake when a vehicle is speeding out of control. Or they forget to simply turn off the ignition.

Something people rarely do is check for a spare and jack when they rent a car. You may find it isn't there when you need it—or that the rental company tries to charge you if the equipment is not there when you return the car.

It should be obvious that you should not leave any financial information or credit cards in your vehicle. Several million cars a year are stolen or broken into.

The following list is more than most of us will carry in our vehicle. Go through the list and select items that suit your circumstances and weather conditions.

National, regional, and metro maps—besides your GPS.

Spare tire, jack, and tire wrench.

Tire inflation canister.

Flashlights: small pen type and large multibattery type. I have the penlight in the glove compartment and the policeman's large type handy in case it is needed in an emergency. I make sure it is not in a position where it can get under my feet and the brake pedal.

Spare fuses. Sometimes there are spares in fuse boxes. Besides having spares, understand how they are replaced.

Warm blankets kept clean in a trash bag in the trunk of the car. It is amazing how many people who live in cold climates freeze to death each year when their cars get stuck in blizzards. Even deserts tend to be very cold during winter. Consider buying emergency thermal blankets. These blankets, available over the Internet and in sporting goods stores, are cheap and are very small when packed, some no bigger than a pack of cigarettes.

Weather sensitive items.

> Winter: a bag with gloves, blanket, cheap plastic rain ponchos, ice scraper, and spray-on ice remover. Some people carry a sack of sand or cat litter to use in case their tires get stuck.

> Summer: drinking water, rain ponchos

> Make sure your engine coolant matches your climate conditions.

> Use windshield wiper spray that removes ice in winter. If you live in regions where snow is rare but rain is not, use wiper spray that helps keep your windows clear during downpours.

Energy bars. Some people carry these—but not if they live in a warm climate where the bars turn to mud in a hot car.

Spare windshield wipers. I had a wiper blade go bad during a recent rainstorm and had to pull off the freeway and change it to keep the window from being scratched. I had a spare because I keep my old usable blades as temporary spares.

Small, briefcase-size umbrella.

Electric tape and duct tape. A common problem in cars is sudden leaks in coolant hoses. The tape can make a shaky but minimally effective patch job.

Auto club membership card—photocopied front and back. (You need your card, too, but most of us carry it because we have more than one car.)

Driver's license—photocopy. I don't include this in my car, but some people do. I leave it out of the car because it contains more personal information than I want a thief to acquire if the car gets broken into.

N95 dust masks. These take up almost no room and will come in handy in an emergency involving an airborne threat. See the discussion of masks in the Protective Masks chapter.

Strong tie-down twine.

First-aid kit.

Battery-operated cell phone recharger.

Pencil/pen and small notepad. These come in handy at the scene of an accident or when you are getting the number of the car that is speeding away with teeth marks on its bumper.

Phone number list.

AM/FM portable radio. Your car is equipped with one, but you can't use it if your battery is dead, a radio fuse is blown, or you have to leave your car.

Multifunction Swiss army–type knife.

Multifunction tool.

Battery cables and/or instant battery starter.

Fire extinguisher (type carried in vehicles).

Battery-operated emergency signal and/or flares.

Compass—besides use of your GPS.

Camera, the disposable type. Toss one in your glove compartment. When a friend who borrowed my car called on her cell phone to tell me another vehicle had hit her, I told her to grab the camera and take pictures. Those pictures reversed an initial insurance company finding that she was at fault.

This occurred before cell phones with cameras (and GPS) became standard equipment for most of us.

As I note later, a cell phone is the most versatile single piece of survival equipment I know of.

16

PROTECTIVE MASKS

N95 MASKS AND
ESCAPE HOODS

Most of the items in survival kits are common household items—
food, a battery-operated radio and other items for a grab-and-go
bag, plastic sheeting and duct tape for a safe room, and so forth.

Protective masks take us into another realm, but one that is
easily dealt with.

The bottom line on protective masks is that you should get
the best one available to fit your pocketbook, exposure, and paranoia.

The most readily available and least expensive protective face
covering is the clothes we are wearing at the time of the incident. Protecting our breathing with a shirt, blouse, or handkerchief is our quickest line of defense. This type of protection falls
under the axiom that something is better than nothing . . .

A T-shirt or handkerchief can offer a little momentary protection from some airborne hazards (biological and radioactive materials big enough to be stopped by the cloth), but they may offer
no protection against others (like gases). In all probability, we
will not know what hazard we are facing; most of us will resort

to using whatever is at hand to try and protect our breathing— hopefully without wasting a moment of getting solid walls between us and the hazard.

The simple cloth masks I have seen sold in the cold-remedies sections of drugstores offer little more protection than a T-shirt. They serve their purpose but are not designed to protect against most of the airborne hazards generated by dirty bombs and chemical eruptions.

The next step up are N95 masks. These are essentially good quality "dust" masks, the type used by many craftsmen when sanding. However, do not confuse these masks with less expensive masks also used by home craftsmen. At the time this was written, N95 masks were marked as such and were available at my local discount hardware store for less than three dollars each. The cheaper masks sell for much less.

Some pharmacies have begun carrying the N95 masks next to the masks typically sold for people trying to avoid catching a cold or the flu. Check the mask's box for hazards covered—the N95 masks are usually superior to the typical cold-flu masks.

The N95 is recommended for home protection because it offers some brief protection from airborne hazards that are dust-like or of a size large enough to be blocked by the masks (for example, some radiological hazards and bacteria). They would not offer protection against many chemical compounds, vapors, and gases, including nerve gas like sarin.

Bottom line: N95 masks are cheap, readily available at your local stores, don't take up much space, and are easy to use. They offer protection from some hazards and fall well within the better-than-nothing category. I have a supply of them and suggest everyone else have them, too.

You should visit a well-stocked hardware store and take a look at the various masks. For more money, there are better masks than the N95.

From the minimal N95, we jump to "escape hoods." These are also called smoke hoods and various other names. Basically, they look like the pullover hood of a winter jacket—but they have a clear plastic face so you can see and a device for filtering air. In an emergency, you grab your hood, pull it over your head, and secure it airtight around your neck.

Escape hoods are designed to be used to escape from a fire or other airborne hazard. As we all know, the biggest killer in fires is usually the incapacitating smoke. Many more people would escape fires if they were not downed by smoke. With a hood on, you can still see and breathe. These hoods are part of the outfit worn by rescue workers, such as firemen.

There are a large number of these hoods on the market and the Internet has many Web sites selling them. They range in price from under a hundred dollars to thousands of dollars. They can only be used once and offer protection for a limited number of hours.

For many of us, the hood would not be an item of interest unless we worked in a high-rise building or in an area where there is a known potential hazard. If I worked in a high-rise, and I have worked in many, I would not be caught dead without one (in a manner of speaking).

Many companies are solicited by their employees to provide these hoods.

If you plan to buy one, remember the old saying about let the buyer beware. I suspect that unless you really research the matter, you could end up with expensive junk. I would be particularly wary of any item advertised as military surplus because they may actually be defective hoods rejected by the military or poor quality knockoffs.

If you can afford it, why not have escape hoods at your office and home? A low-priced but serviceable model may not cost you much more than a ticket to a Broadway play or a game of golf—and may save your life.

17

KI: POTASSIUM
IODIDE

KI, or potassium iodide, is basically an iodine blocker, to help
keep out (or reduce) the impact of iodine on your system. Most
security agency lists recommend having KI tablets on hand.
Even before the threat of terrorism with its grim specter of dirty
bombs, exploding nuclear power plants, and nuclear bombs, KI
was recommended for anyone who lived within miles of a nuclear power plant or was downwind from a plant—and that included a tremendous number of people in this country.

KI is used to help protect against thyroid cancer and other
nasty thyroid problems created by exposure to radioactive materials and fallout—including external exposure, ingesting contaminated food or water, or breathing it in.

Had the people in the regions surrounding the Chernobyl disaster immediately started on KI, their long-term health problems
related to their exposure would have been reduced. Children,
young people, and pregnant women are particularly affected.

KI is not a universal cure-all for radiation poisoning. Specifically, it helps protect against exposure to radioactive isotopes of iodine. Radioactive iodine can become part of the food chain after an accidental or intentional release of radioactive material—it especially affects milk. But you should not delude yourself into believing that you can endure greater exposure to radiation because you take a pill. KI's benefit is to assist with one type of problem, albeit a significant one, and it is only to be used in conjunction with evacuation, sheltering from exposure, and other safeguards.

The instructions and dosage for the use of KI are provided when the product is purchased. The product is designed to be used only in a radiation emergency. Read the instructions and precautions beforehand so you will have a general idea of how to use the product in an emergency situation. There are the usual warnings about waiting for your public health agency to instruct you before taking it, getting medical advice, etc.

The fact that these pills can be purchased without a prescription does not mean they can be used by everyone. Keep in mind that all medications have side effects and KI pills are not safe for everyone.

The Centers for Disease Control and Prevention (CDC) has extensive information about KI pills and I have included information taken from their Web site. Here is the KI information found at www.bt.cdc.gov/radiation/ki.asp and updated as of March 2011.

I have included the information here because access to the Internet may not be available during the crisis.

POTASSIUM IODIDE (KI)

KEY FACTS

- You should only take potassium iodide (KI) on the advice of emergency management officials, public health officials, or your doctor.
- There are health risks associated with taking KI.

What Is Potassium Iodide (KI)?

Potassium iodide (also called KI) is a salt of stable (not radioactive) iodine. Stable iodine is an important chemical needed by the body to make thyroid hormones. Most of the stable iodine in our bodies comes from the food we eat. KI is stable iodine in a medicine form. This fact sheet from the Centers for Disease Control and Prevention (CDC) gives you some basic information about KI. It explains what you should think about before you or a family member takes KI.

What Does KI Do?

Following a radiological or nuclear event, radioactive iodine may be released into the air and then be breathed into the lungs. Radioactive iodine may also contaminate the local food supply and get into the body through food or through drink. When radioactive materials get into the body through breathing, eating, or drinking, we say that "internal contamination" has occurred. In the case of internal contamination with radioactive iodine, the thyroid gland quickly absorbs this chemical. Radioactive iodine absorbed by the thyroid can then injure the gland. Because nonradioactive KI acts to block radioactive iodine from being taken into the thyroid gland, it can help protect this gland from injury.

What Does KI Not Do?

Knowing what KI cannot do is also important. KI cannot prevent radioactive iodine from entering the body. KI can protect only the thyroid from radioactive iodine, not other parts of the body. KI cannot reverse the health effects caused by radioactive iodine once damage to the thyroid has occurred. KI cannot protect the body from radioactive elements other than radioactive iodine—if radioactive iodine is not present, taking KI is not protective.

How Does KI Work?

The thyroid gland cannot tell the difference between stable and radioactive iodine and will absorb both. KI works by blocking radioactive iodine from entering the thyroid. When a person takes KI, the stable iodine in the medicine gets absorbed by the thyroid. Because KI contains so much stable iodine, the thyroid gland becomes "full" and cannot absorb any more iodine—either stable or radioactive—for the next twenty-four hours.

Iodized table salt also contains iodine; iodized table salt contains enough iodine to keep most people healthy under normal conditions. However, table salt does not contain enough iodine to block radioactive iodine from getting into your thyroid gland. You *should not use table salt as a substitute* for KI.

How Well Does KI Work?

Knowing that KI may not give a person 100 percent protection against radioactive iodine is important. How well KI blocks radioactive iodine depends on

- how much time passes between contamination with radioactive iodine and the taking of KI (the sooner a person takes KI, the better),
- how fast KI is absorbed into the blood, and
- the total amount of radioactive iodine to which a person is exposed.

Who Should Take KI?

The thyroid glands of a fetus and of an infant are most at risk of injury from radioactive iodine. Young children and people with low stores of iodine in their thyroid are also at risk of thyroid injury.

INFANTS (INCLUDING BREAST-FED INFANTS): Infants need to be given the recommended dosage of KI for babies (see How much KI should I take?). The amount of KI that gets into breast milk is not enough to protect breast-fed infants from exposure to radioactive iodine. The proper dose of KI given to a nursing infant will help protect it from radioactive iodine that it breathes in or drinks in breast milk.

CHILDREN: The United States Food and Drug Administration (FDA) recommends that all children internally contaminated with (or likely to be internally contaminated with) radioactive iodine take KI, unless they have known allergies to iodine. Children from newborn to eighteen years of age are the most sensitive to the potentially harmful effects of radioactive iodine.

YOUNG ADULTS: The FDA recommends that young adults (between the ages of eighteen and forty years) internally contaminated with (or likely to be internally contaminated with) radioactive iodine take the recommended dose of KI. Young adults are less sensitive to the effects of radioactive iodine than are children.

PREGNANT WOMEN: Because all forms of iodine cross the placenta, pregnant women should take KI to protect the growing fetus. However, pregnant women should take only one dose of KI following internal contamination with (or likely internal contamination with) radioactive iodine.

BREASTFEEDING WOMEN: Women who are breastfeeding should take only one dose of KI if they have been internally contaminated with (or are likely to be internally contaminated with) radioactive iodine. Because radioactive iodine quickly gets into breast milk, CDC recommends that women internally contaminated with (or likely to be internally contaminated with) radioactive iodine stop breastfeeding and feed their child baby formula or other food if it is available. If breast milk is the only food available for an infant, nursing should continue.

ADULTS: Adults older than forty years should not take KI unless public health or emergency management officials say that contamination with a very large dose of radioactive iodine is expected. Adults older than forty years have the lowest chance of developing thyroid cancer or thyroid injury after contamination with radioactive iodine. They also have a greater chance of having allergic reactions to KI.

When Should I Take KI?

After a radiologic or nuclear event, local public health or emergency management officials will tell the public if KI or other protective actions are needed. For example, public health officials may advise you to remain in your home, school, or place of work (this is known as "shelter-in-place") or to evacuate. You may also be told not to eat some foods and not to drink some beverages until a safe supply can be brought in from outside the affected area. Following the instructions given to you by these authorities can lower the amount of radioactive iodine that enters your body and lower the risk of serious injury to your thyroid gland.

How Much KI Should I Take?

The FDA has approved two different forms of KI—tablets and liquid—that people can take by mouth after a nuclear radiation emergency. Tablets come in two strengths, 130 milligrams (mg) and 65 mg. The tablets are scored so they may be cut into smaller pieces for lower doses. Each milliliter (mL) of the oral liquid solution contains 65 mg of KI. According to the FDA, the following doses are appropriate to take after internal contamination with (or likely internal contamination with) radioactive iodine:

- Adults should take 130 mg (one 130-mg tablet OR two 65-mg tablets OR 2 mL of solution).
- Women who are breastfeeding should take the adult dose of 130 mg.

- Children between three and eighteen years of age should take 65 mg (one 65-mg tablet OR 1 mL of solution). Children who are adult size (greater than or equal to 150 pounds) should take the full adult dose, regardless of their age.

- Infants and children between one month and three years of age should take 32 mg (one-half of a 65-mg tablet OR one-half mL of solution). This dose is for both nursing and non-nursing infants and children.

- Newborns from birth to one month of age should be given 16 mg (one-quarter of a 65-mg tablet OR one-quarter mL of solution). This dose is for both nursing and nonnursing newborn infants.

How Often Should I Take KI?

A single dose of KI protects the thyroid gland for twenty-four hours. A one-time dose at the levels recommended in this fact sheet is usually all that is needed to protect the thyroid gland. In some cases, radioactive iodine might be in the environment for more than twenty-four hours. If that happens, local emergency management or public health officials may tell you to take one dose of KI every twenty-four hours for a few days. You should do this only on the advice of emergency management officials, public health officials, or your doctor. Avoid repeat dosing with KI for pregnant and breastfeeding women and newborn infants. Those individuals may need to be evacuated until levels of radioactive iodine in the environment fall.

Taking a higher dose of KI, or taking KI more often than recommended, does not offer more protection and can cause severe illness or death.

Be aware that taking KI may be harmful for some people because of the high levels of iodine in this medicine. You should not take KI if

- you know you are allergic to iodine (If you are unsure about this, consult your doctor. A seafood or shellfish allergy does not necessarily mean that you are allergic to iodine.), or

- you have certain skin disorders (such as dermatitis herpetiformis or urticarial vasculitis).

People with thyroid disease (for example, multinodular goiter, Graves' disease, or autoimmune thyroiditis) may be treated with KI. This should happen under careful supervision of a doctor, especially if dosing lasts for more than a few days.

In all cases, talk to your doctor if you are not sure whether to take KI.

What Are the Possible Risks and Side Effects of KI?

When public health or emergency management officials tell the public to take KI following a radiologic or nuclear event, the benefits of taking this drug outweigh the risks. This is true for all age groups. Some general side effects caused by KI may include intestinal upset, allergic reactions (possibly severe), rashes, and inflammation of the salivary glands.

When taken as recommended, KI causes only rare adverse health effects that specifically involve the thyroid gland. In general, you are more likely to have an adverse health effect involving the thyroid gland if you

- take a higher than recommended dose of KI,
- take the drug for several days, or
- have preexisting thyroid disease.

Newborn infants (less than one month old) who receive more than one dose of KI are at particular risk for developing a condition known as hypothyroidism (thyroid hormone levels that are too low). If not treated, hypothyroidism can cause brain damage. Infants who receive KI should have their thyroid hormone levels checked and monitored by a doctor. Avoid repeat dosing of KI to newborns.

Where Can I Get KI?

KI is available without a prescription. You should talk to your pharmacist to get KI and for directions about how to take it correctly. Your pharmacist can sell you KI brands that have been approved by the FDA.

Where Can I Get More Information About KI?

Other sources of information include:

- The FDA recommendations on KI can be reviewed on the Internet at Frequently Asked Questions on Potassium Iodide (KI).
- The Centers for Disease Control and Prevention's Emergency Response Site is available at CDC Radiation Emergencies.

18

EMERGENCY ELECTRONICS

My personal electronics emergency equipment consists of two
categories: cellular phones and portable radios.

I have resisted owning a GPS because *everyone* I know who
relies upon their GPS appears to me to have lost their instinc-
tual sense of direction. Or, if they haven't lost it, they have
stopped using it. However, I consider a GPS to be a valuable
emergency device even if I will not use one on a daily basis.

GPS is also commonly available with smart phones.

The ordinary cellular phone is the best emergency device
available. Whatever you do, don't leave home without your cell
phone. (Just think about the times you have heard news stories
of people buried beneath buildings collapsed by earthquakes
phoning out to rescuers.) While there are situations in which
your cell phone won't work (such as during a blackout or when
the system is swamped), they do the job most of the time.

Your portable radio, battery or hand cranked, is also a must.
You need at least two them: one in your grab-and-go bag and one

in your safe room bag. These radios are cheap, so have a couple around with an extra battery or two.

A more specialized form of emergency information is the National Oceanic and Atmospheric Administration (NOAA) emergency warning system. Information drawn from the Internet describing the expanded NOAA system follows.

All Hazards NOAA Weather Radios operate off a special broadcast band. NOAA (pronounced *no*-ah) originally broadcast only weather and other natural disaster emergencies, but has been expanded to also include terrorist attacks and technological accidents (chemical spills, nuclear power plant emergencies, train derailments, etc.).

A NOAA radio somewhat resembles a small walkie-talkie. However, for under a hundred dollars, there are also portable sets available that have broadcast bands for AM, FM, NOAA, and the audio output of some TV channels.

Do you need a NOAA radio over and above your AM/FM? If you live in an area with tornadoes and hurricanes, it's a good idea. As for other disasters, I am not convinced that our government would be any more on top of a chemical or other spill than regular radio news broadcasts. But if you can afford it, get one with the multiple bands. If a shortwave band is included in your radio, during the right atmospheric conditions, you can pick up stations from around the world (and some broadcasts are in English even if they are broadcasting from Tokyo or Vienna).

Two-way radios that you can use to send and receive are also plentiful on the market. For those who are really ambitious, some ham radios can send and receive over thousands of miles.

At the time of this writing, FEMA had launched a study to determine whether cell phones, pagers, and network-connected personal digital assistants (PDAs) should be included in the existing Emergency Alert System (EAS). If there was a natural or other disaster in your area, once the system was in operation, you would get a text message.

19

FEDERAL SECURITY GUIDES

Many governmental agencies (federal, state, and local) have a duty to provide information to the public concerning catastrophic dangers such as accidents at chemical facilities and nuclear power plants, terrorist attacks, and natural disasters.

Some of these agencies publish guides or manuals covering a wide range of topics. The FEMA (Federal Emergency Management Agency) *Are You Ready?* publication included in this book is the mother of all emergency planning and survival agency booklets.

Included hereafter are Web addresses for such significant guides and information sources. Some security publications are not included here because they are covered by copyright, including publications of the Red Cross, scouting entities, and even some private studies. However, I did not see information in any of these studies that was not adequately covered by governmental security agencies (which are the source for most of the private works) or my own observations.

Most of these publications are available on the Internet and/ or can be purchased.

My research of survival information turned up a few surprises. For example, when I began the research I did not realize that the CDC (Center for Disease Control and Prevention, part of the Department of Health and Human Services) would have valuable information. The same is true of unlikely candidates for security information such as the Department of Agriculture (USDA), State Department, and others.

I was surprised also by how little usable information was provided by the Federal Bureau of Investigation (FBI) and Department of Justice (DOJ). Rather amazingly, the most valuable information from the Department of Justice Web site, which is essentially the nation's federal police (FBI) and prosecutorial (U.S. Attorney General) agency, was reprinted from a newspaper.

The Department of Justice, FBI, and Bureau of Alcohol, Tobacco, Firearms and Explosives (ATF) might believe that it is the duty of Homeland Security and FEMA to provide this information. But that ignores the point that these agencies can provide information from their unique and well-qualified points of view. The State Department, for example, provides good insights for security on foreign travel.

The Nuclear Regulatory Commission (NRC) dismally fails in its duty to provide information to the public about the dangers of nuclear reactors and survival tactics to minimize the dangers. Nor is it user friendly to those trying to uncover answers about the dangers. It appears obvious that the agency intentionally deceives the public about the dangers of these monstrous threats to our well-being. (Please note: I do not oppose nuclear reactors, I oppose nuclear stupidity and lack of nuclear safety and security.)

Though the security publications can be faulted for sometimes being overcomplicated, for sometimes being written in bureaucratic language that makes it difficult to understand minor points, and for not covering all the territory they should (not even FEMA's), overall, the information provided is extremely valuable.

For that reason, the information I considered most valuable after analyzing the materials were summarized and condensed in the earlier parts of this book.

The following is a list of the survival publications used in writing this book and the Web sites of the agencies who prepared them that can be viewed for updating. You will also find more lists of Web sites that include some other agencies throughout the FEMA *Are You Ready?* publication. I included a link to the Department of Justice's copy of the al-Qaeda terrorist training manual just to remind you what sick, demented creatures terrorists are. The Department of Justice Web site itself does not include the whole manual because it contains brutal details on how to make bombs and kill people.

Are You Ready? (FEMA)	www.fema.gov
Get Ready (DHS)	www.dhs.gov and www.ready.gov
Center for Disease Control	www.cdc.gov and www.cdc.gov/niosh
Emergency Food Safety (USDA)	www.usda.gov
General Food Safety (FSIS)	www.usda.gov and www.fsis.usda.gov
Vulnerable Zones (EPA)	www.epa.gov
Travel Safety (Department of State)	www.travel.state.gov
Nuclear Reactors (NRC)	www.nrc.gov
Homeland Security Advisory System	www.dhs.gov
FBI	www.fbi.gov
State Agencies	www.ready.gov
DOJ: Al-Qaeda Terrorism Manual	www.justice.gov/ag/ manualpart1_1.pdf

The Web sites of the Citizen Corps (http://citizencorps.gov) and the Red Cross (www.redcross.org) both also have valuable information, although most of the material can be found in the sites above.

FEMA GUIDE

This next section is the most relevant information from the comprehensive *Are You Ready?* guide prepared by FEMA. In many cases there are addresses for Web sites giving even more information. Some links found in the online version of the guide have changed and thus have been omitted here. In most cases, if the particular link is no longer available, information can still be found through the Web site's search option.

ARE YOU READY?
AN IN-DEPTH GUIDE TO
CITIZEN PREPAREDNESS

TABLE OF CONTENTS

Why Prepare

Part 1: Basic Preparedness

Section 1.1 Getting Informed

Section 1.2 Emergency Planning and Checklists

Section 1.3 Assemble a Disaster Supplies Kit

Section 1.4 Shelter

Section 1.5 Hazard-Specific Preparedness

Section 1.6 Practicing and Maintaining Your Plan

Part 2: Natural Hazards

Section 2.1 Floods

Section 2.2 Tornadoes

Section 2.3 Hurricanes

Section 2.4 Thunderstorms and Lightning

Section 2.5 Winter Storms and Extreme Cold

Section 2.6 Extreme Heat

Section 2.7 Earthquakes

Section 2.8 Volcanoes

Section 2.9 Landslides and Debris Flows (Mud Slides)

Section 2.10 Tsunamis

Section 2.11 Fires

Section 2.12 Wildfires

Part 3: Technological Hazards

Section 3.1 Hazardous Materials Incidents

Section 3.2 Household Chemical Emergencies

Section 3.3 Nuclear Power Plants

Part 4: Terrorism

Section 4.1 General Information About Terrorism

Section 4.2 Explosions

Section 4.3 Biological Threats

Section 4.4 Chemical Threats

Section 4.5 Nuclear Blasts

Section 4.6 Radiological Dispersion Devices (RDD)

Section 4.7 Homeland Security Advisory System

Part 5: Recovering from Disaster

Appendix A: Water Conservation Tips

Appendix B: Disaster Supplies Checklist

Appendix C: Family Communications Plan

WHY PREPARE

There are real benefits to being prepared.

- Being prepared can reduce fear, anxiety, and losses that accompany disasters. Communities, families, and individuals
should know what to do in the event of a fire and where to

seek shelter during a tornado. They should be ready to evacuate their homes and take refuge in public shelters and know how to care for their basic medical needs.

- People also can reduce the impact of disasters (flood proofing, elevating a home or moving a home out of harm's way, and securing items that could shake loose in an earthquake) and sometimes avoid the danger completely.

The need to prepare is real.

- Disasters disrupt hundreds of thousands of lives every year. Each disaster has lasting effects, both to people and property.

- If a disaster occurs in your community, local government and disaster-relief organizations will try to help you, but you need to be ready as well. Local responders may not be able to reach you immediately, or they may need to focus their efforts elsewhere.

- You should know how to respond to severe weather or any disaster that could occur in your area—hurricanes, earthquakes, extreme cold, flooding, or terrorism.

- You should also be ready to be self-sufficient for at least three days. This may mean providing for your own shelter, first aid, food, water, and sanitation. Using this guide makes preparation practical.

- This guide was developed by the Federal Emergency Management Agency (FEMA), which is the agency responsible for responding to national disasters and for helping state and local governments and individuals prepare for emergencies. It contains step-by-step advice on how to prepare for, respond to, and recover from disasters.

- Used in conjunction with information and instructions from local emergency management offices and the American Red Cross, *Are You Ready?* will give you what you need to be prepared.

Are You Ready? An In-depth Guide to Citizen Preparedness is organized to help you through the process. Begin by reading Part 1, which is the core of the guide. This part provides basic information that is common to all hazards on how to create and maintain an emergency plan and a disaster supplies kit.

PART 1: BASIC PREPAREDNESS

- A series of worksheets to help you obtain information from the community that will form the foundation of your plan. You will need to find out about hazards that threaten the community, how the population will be warned, evacuation routes to be used in times of disaster, and the emergency plans of the community and others that will impact your plan.
- Guidance on specific content that you and your family will need to develop and include in your plan on how to escape from your residence, communicate with one another during times of disaster, shut off household utilities, insure against financial loss, acquire basic safety skills, address special needs such as disabilities, take care of animals, and seek shelter.
- Checklists of items to consider including in your disaster supplies kit that will meet your family's needs following a disaster whether you are at home or at other locations.

Part 1 is also the gateway to the specific hazards and recovery information contained in Parts 2, 3, 4, and 5. Information from these sections should be read carefully and integrated into your emergency plan and disaster supplies kit based on the hazards that pose a threat to you and your family.

PART 2: NATURAL HAZARDS

- Floods
- Tornadoes

- Hurricanes
- Thunderstorms and lightning
- Winter storms and extreme cold
- Extreme heat
- Earthquakes
- Volcanoes
- Landslides and debris flow (mud slides)
- Tsunamis
- Fires
- Wildfires

PART 3: TECHNOLOGICAL HAZARDS

- Hazardous materials incidents
- Household chemical emergencies
- Nuclear power plant emergencies

PART 4: TERRORISM

- Explosions
- Biological threats
- Chemical threats
- Nuclear blasts
- Radiological dispersion device events

PART 5: RECOVERING FROM DISASTER

- Health and safety guidelines
- Returning home
- Seeking disaster assistance
- Coping with disaster
- Helping others

REFERENCES

As you work through individual sections, you will see reference points. These are reminders to refer to previous sections for related information on the topic being discussed.

FEMA Publications

Throughout the guide are lists of publications available from FEMA that can help you learn more about the topics covered. To obtain these publications, call the FEMA Distribution Center at (800) 480-2520 or request them by mail from:

> Federal Emergency Management Agency
> P.O. Box 2012
> Jessup, MD 20794-2012

Other Publications

Other publications cited throughout this guide can be obtained by contacting the organizations below:

> American Red Cross National Headquarters
> 2025 E Street, NW
> Washington, DC 20006
> (202) 303-4498
> www.redcross.org

> National Weather Service
> 1325 East West Highway
> Silver Spring, MD 20910
> www.nws.noaa.gov/education.html

> Centers for Disease Control and Prevention
> 1600 Clifton Road
> Atlanta, GA 30333
> (404) 639-3534 or (800) 311-3435
> www.cdc.gov

U.S. Geological Survey
Information Services
P.O. Box 25286
Denver, CO 80225
(888) 275-8747
www.usgs.gov

Disaster Public Education Web Sites

You can broaden your knowledge of disaster preparedness topics presented in this guide by reviewing information provided at various governmental and nongovernmental Web sites. Provided below is a list of recommended sites. The Web address for each site reflects its home address. Searches conducted from each home site's page result in the most current and extensive list of available material for the site.

Governmental Sites

Be Ready Campaign—www.ready.gov

Agency for Toxic Substances and Disease Registry—www .atsdr.cdc.gov

Centers for Disease Control and Prevention—www.cdc.gov

Citizen Corps—www.citizencorps.gov

Department of Commerce—www.doc.gov

Department of Education—www.ed.gov

Department of Energy—www.energy.gov

Department of Health and Human Services—www.hhs .gov/disasters

Department of Homeland Security—www.dhs.gov

Department of Interior—www.doi.gov

Department of Justice—www.justice.gov

Environmental Protection Agency—www.epa.gov

Federal Emergency Management Agency—www.fema.gov

Food and Drug Administration—www.fda.gov

National Oceanic and Atmospheric Administration—www
.noaa.gov

National Weather Service—www.nws.noaa.gov

Nuclear Regulatory Commission—www.nrc.gov

U.S. Department of Agriculture—www.usda.gov

U.S. Fire Administration—www.usfa.fema.gov

U.S. Fire Administration Kids Page—www.usfa.fema.gov
/kids

U.S. Geological Survey—www.usgs.gov

U.S. Office of Personnel Management—www.opm.gov

U.S. Postal Service—www.usps.gov

USDA Forest Service Southern Research Station—www
.wildfireprograms.com

White House—www.whitehouse.gov

Nongovernmental Sites

American Red Cross—www.redcross.org

Institute for Business and Home Safety—www.ibhs.org

National Fire Protection Association—www.nfpa.org

National Mass Fatalities Institute—www.nmfi.org

National Safety Compliance—www.osha-safety-training.net

Middle East Seismological Forum—www.meseisforum.net

Pan American Health Organization—www.disaster-info.net /SUMA

PART 1: BASIC PREPAREDNESS

In this part of the guide, you will learn preparedness strategies that are common to all disasters. You plan only once, and are able to apply your plan to all types of hazards.

When you complete Part 1, you will be able to:

- get informed about hazards and emergencies that may affect you and your family;
- develop an emergency plan;
- collect and assemble a disaster supplies kit;
- learn where to seek shelter from all types of hazards;
- identify the community warning systems and evacuation routes;
- include in your plan required information from community and school plans;
- learn what to do for specific hazards;
- practice and maintain your plan.

1.1. GETTING INFORMED

Learn about the hazards that may strike your community, the risks you face from these hazards, and your community's plans for warning and evacuation. You can obtain this information from your local emergency management office or your local chapter of the American Red Cross. Space has been provided here to record your answers.

Hazards

Ask local authorities about each possible hazard or emergency and use the worksheet that follows to record your findings and suggestions for reducing your family's risk.

POSSIBLE HAZARDS/ EMERGENCIES	RISK LEVEL (NONE, LOW, MODERATE, OR HIGH)	HOW CAN I REDUCE MY RISK?

NATURAL HAZARDS

1. Floods   ____   _____
2. Hurricanes   ____   _____
3. Thunderstorms and lightning   ____   _____
4. Tornadoes   ____   _____
5. Winter storms and extreme cold   ____   _____
6. Extreme heat   ____   _____
7. Earthquakes   ____   _____
8. Volcanoes   ____   _____
9. Landslides and debris flow   ____   _____
10. Tsunamis   ____   _____
11. Fires   ____   _____
12. Wildfires   ____   _____

TECHNOLOGICAL HAZARDS

1. Hazardous materials incidents   ____   _____
2. Nuclear power plants incidents   ____

TERRORISM

1. Explosions ____ _____
2. Biological threats ____ _____
3. Chemical threats ____ _____
4. Nuclear blasts ____ _____
5. Radiological
   dispersion
   device (RDD) ____ _____

You also can consult FEMA for hazard maps for your area. Go to www.fema.gov, select maps, and follow the directions.

Warning Systems and Signals

The Emergency Alert System (EAS) can address the entire nation on very short notice in case of a grave threat or national emergency. Ask if your local radio and TV stations participate in the EAS.

National Oceanic and Atmospheric Administration (NOAA) Weather Radio (NWR) is a nationwide network of radio stations broadcasting continuous weather information directly from a nearby National Weather Service office to specially configured NOAA weather radio receivers. Determine if NOAA Weather Radio is available where you live. If so, consider purchasing a NOAA weather radio receiver. Ask local authorities about methods used to warn your community.

NOTE: What action you should take will depend upon the warning given by the system.

Evacuating Yourself and Your Family

When community evacuations become necessary, local officials provide information to the public through the media. In some circumstances, other warning methods, such as sirens or telephone calls, also are used. Additionally, there may be circumstances under which you and your family feel threatened or endangered and you need to leave your home, school, or workplace to avoid these situations. The amount of time you have to leave will depend on the hazard. If the event is a weather condition, such as a hurricane that can be monitored, you might have a day or two to get ready. However, many disasters allow no time for people to gather even the most basic necessities, which is why planning ahead is essential.

Evacuation: More Common Than You Realize

Evacuations are more common than many people realize. Hundreds of times each year, transportation and industrial accidents release harmful substances, forcing thousands of people to leave their homes. Fires and floods cause evacuations even more frequently. Almost every year, people along the Gulf and Atlantic coasts evacuate in the face of approaching hurricanes.

Ask local authorities about emergency evacuation routes. Record your specific evacuation route directions in the space provided.

Is there a map available with evacuation routes marked?

____ Yes   ____ No

Community and Other Plans

Ask local officials the following questions about your community's disaster/emergency plans.

Does my community have a plan?   ____ Yes   ____ No

Can I obtain a copy?   ____ Yes   ____ No

What does the plan contain?

How often is it updated?

What should I know about the plan?

What hazards does it cover?

EVACUATION GUIDELINES

Always

Keep a full tank of gas in your car if an evacuation seems likely. Gas stations may be closed during emergencies and unable to pump gas during power outages. Plan to take one car per family to reduce congestion and delay.

Make transportation arrangements with friends or your local government if you do not own a car.

Listen to a battery-powered radio and follow local evacuation instructions.

Gather your family and go if you are instructed to evacuate immediately.

Leave early enough to avoid being trapped by severe weather.

Follow recommended evacuation routes. Do not take shortcuts; they may be blocked.

Be alert for washed-out roads and bridges. Do not drive into flooded areas.

Stay away from downed power lines.

If Time Permits

Gather your disaster supplies kit.

Wear sturdy shoes and clothing that provides some protection, such as long pants, long-sleeved shirts, and a cap.

Secure your home:

- Close and lock doors and windows.
- Unplug electrical equipment, such as radios and televisions, and small appliances, such as toasters and microwaves. Leave freezers and refrigerators plugged in unless there is a risk of flooding.

Let others know where you are going.

In addition to finding out about your community's plan, it is important that you know what plans are in place for your workplace and your children's school or day care center.

- Ask your employer about workplace policies regarding disasters and emergencies, including understanding how you will be provided with emergency and warning information.
- Contact your children's school or day care center to discuss their disaster procedures.

School Emergency Plans

Know your children's school emergency plan:

- Ask how the school will communicate with families during a crisis.
- Ask if the school stores adequate food, water, and other basic supplies.
- Find out if the school is prepared to shelter-in-place if need be, and where they plan to go if they must get away.

In cases where schools institute procedures to shelter-in-place, you may not be permitted to drive to the school to pick up your children. Even if you go to the school, the doors will likely be locked to keep your children safe. Monitor local media outlets for announcements about changes in school openings and closings, and follow the directions of local emergency officials.

For more information on developing emergency preparedness plans for schools, please log on to the U.S. Department of Education at www.ed.gov/emergencyplan.

Workplace Plans

If you are an employer, make sure your workplace has a building evacuation plan that is regularly practiced.

- Take a critical look at your heating, ventilation, and air-conditioning system to determine if it is secure or if it could feasibly be upgraded to better filter potential contaminants, and be sure you know how to turn it off if you need to.

- Think about what to do if your employees can't go home.
- Make sure you have appropriate supplies on hand.

1.2. EMERGENCY PLANNING AND CHECKLISTS

Now that you've learned about what can happen and how your community is prepared to respond to emergencies, prepare your family by creating a family disaster plan. You can begin this process by gathering family members and reviewing the information you obtained in section 1.1, Getting Informed (hazards, warning systems, evacuation routes, and community and other plans). Discuss with them what you would do if family members are not home when a warning is issued. Additionally, your family plan should address the following:

- Escape routes.
- Family communications.
- Utility shut-off and safety.
- Insurance and vital records.
- Special needs.
- Caring for animals.
- Safety skills.

Information on these family-planning considerations are covered in the following sections.

Escape Routes

Draw a floor plan of your home. Use a blank sheet of paper for each floor. Mark two escape routes from each room. Make sure children understand the drawings. Post a copy of the drawings at eye level in each child's room.

Where to Meet

Establish a place to meet in the event of an emergency, such as a fire. Record the locations below:

Near the home (for example, the next door neighbor's telephone pole)

Outside the immediate area (for example, the neighborhood grocery store parking lot)

Family Communications

Your family may not be together when disaster strikes, so plan how you will contact one another. Think about how you will communicate in different situations.

Complete a contact card for each family member. Have family members keep these cards handy in a wallet, purse, backpack, etc. You may want to send one to school with each child to keep on file. Pick a friend or relative who lives out of state for household members to notify that they are safe.

Copies of contact cards to fill out can be found in Appendix C. Also in Appendix C is a more detailed family communications plan that should be completed and posted so the contact information is readily accessible to all family members. A copy should also be included in your family disaster supplies kit.

Utility Shut-off and Safety

In the event of a disaster, you may be instructed to shut off the utility service at your home.

The following is some general guidance for shutting off utility service. Modify the information provided to reflect your shut-off requirements as directed by your utility company(ies).

Natural Gas

Natural gas leaks and explosions are responsible for a significant number of fires following disasters. It is vital that all household members know how to shut off natural gas.

Because there are different gas shut-off procedures for different gas meter configurations, it is important to contact your local gas company for guidance on preparation and response regarding gas appliances and gas service to your home.

When you learn the proper shut-off procedure for your meter, share the information with everyone in your household. Be sure not to actually turn off the gas when practicing the proper gas shut-off procedure.

If you smell gas or hear a blowing or hissing noise, open a window and get everyone out quickly. Turn off the gas, using the outside main valve if you can, and call the gas company from a neighbor's home.

Caution: If you turn off the gas for any reason, a qualified professional must turn it back on. *Never* attempt to turn the gas back on yourself.

Water

Water quickly becomes a precious resource following many disasters. It is vital that all household members learn how to shut off the water at the main house valve.

- Cracked lines may pollute the water supply to your house. It is wise to shut off your water until you hear from authorities that it is safe for drinking.
- The effects of gravity may drain the water in your hot water heater and toilet tanks unless you trap it in your house by shutting off the main house valve (not the street valve in the cement box at the curb—this valve is extremely difficult to turn and requires a special tool).

PREPARING TO SHUT OFF WATER

Locate the shut-off valve for the water line that enters your house.

Note: Everyone should know how to turn off their water, gas and electrical service into their residence. If you don't know how to do it, ask someone with knowledge. Some information is also available on the Internet version of this guide.

- Make sure this valve can be completely shut off. Your valve may be rusted open, or it may only partially close. Replace it if necessary.
- Label this valve with a tag for easy identification, and make sure all household members know where it is located.

Electricity

Electrical sparks have the potential to ignite natural gas if it is leaking. It is wise to teach all responsible household members where and how to shut off the electricity.

PREPARING TO SHUT OFF ELECTRICITY

- Locate your electricity circuit box.
- Teach all responsible household members how to shut off the electricity to the entire house.

For your safety: Always shut off all the individual circuits before shutting off the main circuit breaker.

Insurance and Vital Records

Obtain property, health, and life insurance if you do not have them. Review existing policies for the amount and extent of coverage to ensure that what you have in place is what is required for you and your family for all possible hazards.

Flood Insurance

If you live in a flood-prone area, consider purchasing flood insurance to reduce your risk of flood loss. Buying flood insurance to cover the value of a building and its contents will not only provide greater peace of mind, but will speed the recovery if a flood occurs. You can call (888) FLOOD29 to learn more about flood insurance.

Inventory Home Possessions

Make a record of your personal property, for insurance purposes. Take photos or a video of the interior and exterior of your home. Include personal belongings in your inventory.

You may also want to download the free *Household and Personal Property Inventory Book* from the University of Illinois at www.ag.uiuc.edu/~vista/abstracts/ahouseinv.html to help you record your possessions.

Important Documents

Store important documents such as insurance policies, deeds, property records, and other important papers in a safe place, such as a safety deposit box away from your home. Make copies of important documents for your disaster supplies kit. (Information about the disaster supplies kit is covered later.)

Money

Consider saving money in an emergency savings account that could be used in any crisis. It is advisable to keep a small amount of cash or traveler's checks at home in a safe place where you can quickly access them in case of evacuation.

Special Needs

If you or someone close to you has a disability or a special need, you may have to take additional steps to protect yourself and your family in an emergency.

DISABILITY/SPECIAL NEEDS

_____ Hearing impaired/May need to make special arrangements to receive warnings.

_____ Mobility impaired/May need special assistance to get to a shelter.

_____ Single working parent/May need help to plan for disasters and emergencies.

_____ Non-English-speaking persons/May need assistance planning for and responding to emergencies. Community and cultural groups may be able to help keep people informed.

_____ People without vehicles/May need to make arrangements for transportation.

_____ People with special dietary needs/Should take special precautions to have an adequate emergency food supply.

Planning for Special Needs

If you have special needs:

- Find out about special assistance that may be available in your community. Register with the office of emergency services or the local fire department for assistance so needed help can be provided.
- Create a network of neighbors, relatives, friends, and co-workers to aid you in an emergency. Discuss your needs

and make sure everyone knows how to operate necessary equipment.

- Discuss your needs with your employer.
- If you are mobility impaired and live or work in a high-rise building, have an escape chair.
- If you live in an apartment building, ask the management to mark accessible exits clearly and to make arrangements to help you leave the building.
- Keep specialized items ready, including extra wheelchair batteries, oxygen, catheters, medication, food for service animals, and any other items you might need.
- Be sure to make provisions for medications that require refrigeration.
- Keep a list of the type and model numbers of the medical devices you require.

Caring for Animals

Animals also are affected by disasters. Know that, with the exception of service animals, pets are not typically permitted in emergency shelters as they may affect the health and safety of other occupants. Use the guidelines below to prepare a plan for caring for pets and large animals.

Plan for pet disaster needs by:

- Identifying proper animal shelter.
- Gathering pet supplies.
- Ensuring your pet has proper ID and up-to-date veterinarian records.
- Providing a pet carrier and leash.

Take the following steps to prepare to shelter your pet:

- Call your local emergency management office, animal shelter, or animal control office to get advice and information.

- Keep veterinary records to prove vaccinations are current.
- Find out which local hotels and motels allow pets and where pet boarding facilities are located. Be sure to research some outside your local area in case local facilities close.

Guidelines for Large Animals

If you have large animals such as horses, cattle, sheep, goats, or pigs on your property, be sure to prepare before a disaster. Use the following guidelines:

- Ensure all animals have some form of identification.
- Evacuate animals whenever possible. Map out primary and secondary routes in advance.
- Make available vehicles and trailers needed for transporting and supporting each type of animal. Also make available experienced handlers and drivers. *Note:* It is best to allow animals a chance to become accustomed to vehicular travel so they are less frightened and easier to move.
- Ensure destinations have food, water, veterinary care, and handling equipment.
- If evacuation is not possible, animal owners must decide whether to move large animals to shelter or turn them outside.

Safety Skills

It is important that family members know how to administer first aid and CPR and how to use a fire extinguisher.

Learn First Aid and CPR

Take a first aid and CPR class. Local American Red Cross chapters can provide information about this type of training. Official certification by the American Red Cross provides, under the "good Samaritan" law, protection for those giving first aid.

Learn How to Use a Fire Extinguisher

Be sure everyone knows how to use your fire extinguisher(s) and where it is kept. You should have, at a minimum, an ABC type.

1.3. ASSEMBLE A DISASTER SUPPLIES KIT

You may need to survive on your own after a disaster. This means having your own food, water, and other supplies in sufficient quantity to last for at least three days. Local officials and relief workers will be on the scene after a disaster, but they cannot reach everyone immediately. You could get help in hours, or it might take days.

Basic services such as electricity, gas, water, sewage treatment, and telephones may be cut off for days, or even a week or longer. Or, you may have to evacuate at a moment's notice and take essentials with you. You probably will not have the opportunity to shop or search for the supplies you need.

A disaster supplies kit is a collection of basic items that members of a household may need in the event of a disaster.

Kit Locations

Since you do not know where you will be when an emergency occurs, prepare supplies for home, work, and vehicles.

Home

Your disaster supplies kit should contain essential food, water, and supplies for at least three days.

Keep this kit in a designated place and have it ready in case you have to leave your home quickly. Make sure all family members know where the kit is kept. Additionally, you may want to consider having supplies for sheltering for up to two weeks.

Work

This kit should be in one container, and ready to "grab and go" in case you are evacuated from your workplace. Make sure you have food and water in the kit. Also, be sure to have comfortable walking shoes at your workplace in case an evacuation requires walking long distances.

Car

In case you are stranded, keep a kit of emergency supplies in your car. This kit should contain food, water, first-aid supplies, flares, jumper cables, and seasonal supplies.

How Much Water Do I Need?

You should store at least one gallon of water per person per day. A normally active person needs at least one-half gallon of water daily just for drinking.

Additionally, in determining adequate quantities, take the following into account:

- Individual needs vary, depending on age, physical condition, activity, diet, and climate.
- Children, nursing mothers, and ill people need more water.
- Very hot temperatures can double the amount of water needed.
- A medical emergency might require additional water.

How Should I Store Water?

To prepare the safest and most reliable emergency supply of water, it is recommended you purchase commercially bottled water. Keep bottled water in its original container and do not open it until you need to use it. Observe the expiration or "use by" date.

If You Are Preparing Your Own Containers

It is recommended you purchase food-grade water storage containers from surplus or camping supplies stores to use for water storage. Before filling with water, thoroughly clean the containers with dishwashing soap and water, and rinse completely so there is no residual soap. Follow the directions below on filling the container with water.

If you choose to use your own storage containers, choose two-liter plastic soft-drink bottles—not plastic jugs or cardboard containers that have had milk or fruit juice in them. Milk protein and fruit sugars cannot be adequately removed from these containers and provide an environment for bacterial growth when water is stored in them. Cardboard containers also leak easily and are not designed for long-term storage of liquids. Also, do not use glass containers, because they can break and are heavy.

If storing water in plastic soda bottles, follow these steps:

- Thoroughly clean the bottles with dishwashing soap and water, and rinse completely so there is no residual soap.
- Sanitize the bottles by adding a solution of one teaspoon of nonscented liquid household chlorine bleach to a quart of water. Swish the sanitizing solution in the bottle so that it touches all surfaces. After sanitizing the bottle, thoroughly rinse out the sanitizing solution with clean water.

FILLING WATER CONTAINERS

- Fill the bottle to the top with regular tap water. If the tap water has been commercially treated from a water utility with chlorine, you do not need to add anything else to the water to keep it clean. If the water you are using comes from a well or water source that is not treated with chlorine, add two drops of nonscented liquid household chlorine bleach to the water.

- Tightly close the container using the original cap. Be careful not to contaminate the cap by touching the inside of it with your finger. Place a date on the outside of the container so that you know when you filled it. Store it in a cool, dark place.
- Replace the water every six months if not using commercially bottled water.

Food

The following are things to consider when putting together your food supplies:

- Avoid foods that will make you thirsty. Choose salt-free crackers, whole grain cereals, and canned foods with high liquid content.
- Stock canned foods, dry mixes, and other staples that do not require refrigeration, cooking, water, or special preparation. You may already have many of these on hand. *Note:* Be sure to include a manual can opener.
- Include special dietary needs.

Basic Disaster Supplies Kit

The following items are recommended for inclusion in your basic disaster supplies kit:

- Three-day supply of nonperishable food.
- Three-day supply of water—one gallon of water per person, per day.
- Portable, battery-powered radio or television and extra batteries.

- Flashlight and extra batteries.
- First-aid kit and manual.
- Sanitation and hygiene items (moist towelettes and toilet paper).
- Matches and waterproof container.
- Whistle.
- Extra clothing.
- Kitchen accessories and cooking utensils, including a can opener.
- Photocopies of credit and identification cards.
- Cash and coins.
- Special needs items, such as prescription medications, eyeglasses, contact lens solutions, and hearing-aid batteries.
- Items for infants, such as formula, diapers, bottles, and pacifiers.
- Other items to meet your unique family needs.

If you live in a cold climate, you must think about warmth. It is possible that you will not have heat. Think about your clothing and bedding supplies. Be sure to include one complete change of clothing and pair of shoes per person, including:

- Jacket or coat.
- Long pants.
- Long-sleeve shirt.
- Sturdy shoes.
- Hat, mittens, and scarf.
- Sleeping bag or warm blanket (per person).

Be sure to account for growing children and other family changes. See Appendix B for a detailed checklist of disaster supplies. You may want to add some of the items listed to your basic disaster supplies kit depending on the specific needs of your family.

Maintaining Your Disaster Supplies Kit

Just as important as putting your supplies together is maintaining them so they are safe to use when needed. Here are some tips to keep your supplies ready and in good condition:

- Keep canned foods in a dry place where the temperature is cool.
- Store boxed food in tightly closed plastic or metal containers to protect from pests and to extend its shelf life.
- Throw out any canned good that becomes swollen, dented, or corroded.
- Use foods before they go bad, and replace them with fresh supplies.
- Place new items at the back of the storage area and older ones in the front.
- Change stored food and water supplies every six months. Be sure to write the date you store it on all containers.
- Rethink your needs every year and update your kit as your family needs change.
- Keep items in airtight plastic bags and put your entire disaster supplies kit in one or two easy-to-carry containers, such as an unused trash can, camping backpack, or duffel bag.

1.4. SHELTER

Taking shelter is critical in times of disaster. Sheltering is appropriate when conditions require that you seek protection in your home, place of employment, or other location where you are when disaster strikes. Sheltering outside the hazard area would include staying with friends and relatives, seeking commercial lodging, or staying in a mass care facility operated by disaster relief groups in conjunction with local authorities.

To effectively shelter, you must first consider the hazard and then choose a place in your home or other building that is safe for that hazard. For example, for a tornado, a room should be selected that is in a basement or an interior room on the lowest level away from corners, windows, doors, and outside walls. Because the safest locations to seek shelter vary by hazard, sheltering is discussed in the various hazard sections. These discussions include recommendations for sealing the shelter if the hazard warrants this type of protection.

Even though mass care shelters often provide water, food, medicine, and basic sanitary facilities, you should plan to take your disaster supplies kit with you so you will have the supplies you require. Mass care sheltering can involve living with many people in a confined space, which can be difficult and unpleasant. To avoid conflicts in this stressful situation, it is important to cooperate with shelter managers and others assisting them. Keep in mind that alcoholic beverages and weapons are forbidden in emergency shelters and smoking is restricted.

The length of time you are required to shelter may be short, such as during a tornado warning, or long, such as during a winter storm. It is important that you stay in the shelter until local authorities say it is safe to leave. Additionally, you should take turns listening to radio broadcasts and maintain a twenty-four-hour safety watch.

During extended periods of sheltering, you will need to manage water and food supplies to ensure you and your family have the required supplies and quantities. Guidance on how to accomplish this follows.

Managing Water

Essentials:

- Allow people to drink according to their needs. Many people need even more than the average of one-half gallon per day. The individual amount needed depends on age, physical activity, physical condition, and time of year.

- Never ration water unless ordered to do so by authorities. Drink the amount you need today and try to find more for tomorrow. Under no circumstances should a person drink less than one quart (four cups) of water each day. You can minimize the amount of water your body needs by reducing activity and staying cool.

- Drink water that you know is not contaminated first. If necessary, suspicious water, such as cloudy water from regular faucets or water from streams or ponds, can be used after it has been treated. If water treatment is not possible, put off drinking suspicious water as long as possible, but do not become dehydrated.

- Do not drink carbonated beverages instead of drinking water. Carbonated beverages do not meet drinking-water requirements. Caffeinated drinks and alcohol dehydrate the body, which increases the need for drinking water.

- Turn off the main water valves in your home. You will need to protect the water sources already in your home from contamination if you hear reports of broken water or sewage lines, or if local officials advise you of a problem. To close the incoming water source, locate the incoming valve and turn it to the closed position. Be sure you and other family members know how to perform this important procedure.

  - To use the water in your pipes, let air into the plumbing by turning on the faucet in your home at the highest level. A small amount of water will trickle out. Then obtain water from the lowest faucet in the home.

  - To use the water in your hot-water tank, be sure the electricity or gas is off, and open the drain at the bottom of the tank. Start the water flowing by turning off the water intake valve at the tank and turning on the hot water faucet. Refill the tank before turning the gas or electricity back on. If the gas is turned off, a professional will be needed to turn it back on.

Water Sources

SAFE SOURCES

- Melted ice cubes.
- Water drained from the water heater (if the water heater has not been damaged).
- Liquids from canned goods such as fruit or vegetable juices.
- Water drained from pipes.

UNSAFE SOURCES

- Radiators.
- Hot water boilers (home heating system).
- Water beds (fungicides added to the water or chemicals in the vinyl may make water unsafe to use).
- Water from the toilet bowl or flush tank.
- Swimming pools and spas (chemicals used to kill germs are too concentrated for safe drinking but can be used for personal hygiene, cleaning, and related uses).

Water Treatment

Treat all water of uncertain quality before using it for drinking, food washing or preparation, washing dishes, brushing teeth, or making ice. In addition to having a bad odor and taste, contaminated water can contain microorganisms (germs) that cause diseases such as dysentery, cholera, typhoid, and hepatitis.

There are many ways to treat water. None is perfect. Often the best solution is a combination of methods. Before treating, let any suspended particles settle to the bottom or strain them through coffee filters or layers of clean cloth.

Make sure you have the necessary materials in your disaster supplies kit for the chosen water treatment method.

There are three water treatment methods. They are as follows:

- Boiling
- Chlorination
- Distillation

These instructions are for treating water of uncertain quality in an emergency situation, when no other reliable clean water source is available, or you have used all of your stored water.

BOILING

Boiling is the safest method of treating water. In a large pot or kettle, bring water to a rolling boil for one full minute, keeping in mind that some water will evaporate.

Let the water cool before drinking. Boiled water will taste better if you put oxygen back into it by pouring the water back and forth between two clean containers. This also will improve the taste of stored water.

CHLORINATION

You can use household liquid bleach to kill microorganisms. Use only regular household liquid bleach that contains 5.25 to 6.0 percent sodium hypochlorite. Do not use scented bleaches, color-safe bleaches, or bleaches with added cleaners. Because the potency of bleach diminishes with time, use bleach from a newly opened or unopened bottle.

Add sixteen drops (one-eighth teaspoon) of bleach per gallon of water, stir, and let stand for thirty minutes. The water should have a slight bleach odor. If it doesn't, then repeat the dosage and let stand another fifteen minutes. If it still does not smell of chlorine, discard it and find another source of water.

Other chemicals, such as iodine or water treatment products

sold in camping or surplus stores that do not contain 5.25 to 6.0 percent sodium hypochlorite as the only active ingredient, are not recommended and should not be used.

DISTILLATION

While the two methods described above will kill most microbes in water, distillation will remove microbes (germs) that resist these methods, as well as heavy metals, salts, and most other chemicals.

Distillation involves boiling water and then collecting only the vapor that condenses. The condensed vapor will not include salt or most other impurities. To distill, fill a pot halfway with water. Tie a cup to the handle on the pot's lid so that the cup will hang right-side-up when the lid is upside-down (make sure the cup is not dangling into the water) and boil the water for twenty minutes. The water that drips from the lid into the cup is distilled.

EFFECTIVENESS OF WATER TREATMENT METHODS

Boiling: Kills microbes

Chlorination: Kills microbes

Distillation: Kills microbes; removes other contaminants (heavy metals, salts, and most other chemicals)

Managing Food Supplies

Safety and Sanitation

Do:

- Keep food in covered containers.
- Keep cooking and eating utensils clean.
- Keep garbage in closed containers and dispose outside, burying garbage if necessary.

- Keep your hands clean by washing them frequently with soap and water that has been boiled or disinfected.
- Use only prepepared canned baby formula for infants.
- Discard any food that has come into contact with contaminated floodwater.
- Discard any food that has been at room temperature for two hours or more.
- Discard any food that has an unusual odor, color, or texture.

Don't:

- Eat food from cans that are swollen, dented, or corroded, even though the product may look safe to eat.
- Eat any food that looks or smells abnormal, even if the can looks normal.
- Use powdered formulas with treated water.
- Let garbage accumulate inside, both for fire and sanitation reasons.

Note: Thawed food usually can be eaten if it is still "refrigerator cold." It can be refrozen if it still contains ice crystals. To be safe, remember, "When in doubt, throw it out."

Cooking

- Alternative cooking sources in times of emergency include candle warmers, chafing dishes, fondue pots, or a fireplace.
- Charcoal grills and camp stoves are for outdoor use only.
- Commercially canned food may be eaten out of the can without warming.

TO HEAT FOOD IN A CAN:

1. Remove the label.
2. Thoroughly wash and disinfect the can. (Use a diluted solution of one part bleach to ten parts water.)
3. Open the can before heating.

Managing Without Power

Here are two options for keeping food safe if you are without power for a long period:

1. Look for alternate storage space for your perishable food.
2. Use dry ice. Twenty-five pounds of dry ice will keep a ten-cubic-foot freezer below freezing for three to four days. Use care when handling dry ice, and wear dry, heavy gloves to avoid injury.

1.5. HAZARD-SPECIFIC PREPAREDNESS

There are actions that should be taken before, during, and after an event that are unique to each hazard. For example:

• Seeking a safe shelter during a tornado.
• Reducing property loss from a hurricane.

Information about the specific hazards and what to do for each is provided in Parts 2, 3, and 4. Study the material for those hazards that you identified in section 1.1, Getting Informed, as the ones that have happened or could happen. Share the hazard-specific information with family members and include pertinent material from these parts in your family disaster plan.

1.6. PRACTICING AND MAINTAINING YOUR PLAN

Once you have developed your plan, you need to practice and maintain it. For example, ask questions to make sure your family remembers meeting places, phone numbers, and safety rules. Conduct drills such as drop, cover, and hold on for earthquakes. Test fire alarms. Replace and update disaster supplies.

For More Information

If you require more information about any of these topics, the following are resources that may be helpful.

FEMA Publications

Disaster Preparedness Coloring Book. FEMA-243. Coloring book for ages three to ten. Also available in Spanish.

Before Disaster Strikes. FEMA A-291. Contains information about how to make sure you are financially prepared to deal with a natural disaster. Also available in Spanish.

The Adventures of Julia and Robbie: Disaster Twins. FEMA-344. A collection of disaster-related stories. Includes information on preparedness and how to mitigate against disasters.

FEMA for Kids. L-229. Provides information about what FEMA (specifically fema.gov) has to offer children.

Community Shelter. FEMA 361. Contains guidelines for constructing mass shelters for public refuge in schools, hospitals, and other places.

Food and Water in an Emergency. L-210. If an earthquake, hurricane, winter storm, or other disaster strikes your community, you might not have access to food, water, and electricity for days, or even weeks. By taking some time now to store emergency food and water supplies, you can provide for your entire family. Also available online at www.fema.gov/pdf/library/f&web.pdf.

Helping Children Cope with Disaster. FEMA L-196. Helps families understand how to help children cope with disaster and its aftermath.

Assisting People with Disabilities in a Disaster. Information about helping people with disabilities in a disaster and resources for individuals with disabilities. Available online at www.fema.gov/.

American Red Cross Publication

Facing Fear: Helping Young People Deal with Terrorism and Tragic Events. A school curriculum designed to help alleviate worries and clear up confusion about perceived and actual threats to safety. Available online at www.red cross.org/ contact your local Red Cross chapter.

PART 2: NATURAL HAZARDS

Part 2 includes information about many types of natural hazards. Natural hazards are natural events that threaten lives, property, and other assets. Often, natural hazards can be predicted. They tend to occur repeatedly in the same geographical locations because they are related to weather patterns or physical characteristics of an area.

Natural hazards such as floods, fires, earthquakes, tornadoes, and windstorms affect thousands of people every year. We need to know what our risks are from natural hazards and take sensible precautions to protect ourselves, our families, and our communities.

Use Part 2 to learn about the hazards that pose a risk to you. Include the pertinent information in your family disaster plan. Specific content on each hazard consists of the characteristics of that hazard, terms associated with the hazard, measures that can be taken beforehand to avoid or lessen the impact of these events, and what individuals need to do during and after the event to protect themselves.

When you complete Part 2, you will be able to:

- know important terms;
- take protective measures for natural hazards;
- identify resources for more information about natural hazards.

2.1. FLOODS

Floods are one of the most common hazards in the United States. Flood effects can be local, impacting a neighborhood or community, or very large, affecting entire river basins and multiple states.

However, all floods are not alike. Some floods develop slowly, sometimes over a period of days. But flash floods can develop quickly, sometimes in just a few minutes and without any visible signs of rain. Flash floods often have a dangerous wall of roaring water that carries rocks, mud, and other debris and can sweep away most things in its path. Overland flooding occurs outside a defined river or stream, such as when a levee is breached, but still can be destructive. Flooding can also occur when a dam breaks, producing effects similar to flash floods.

Be aware of flood hazards no matter where you live, but especially if you live in a low-lying area, near water or downstream from a dam. Even very small streams, gullies, creeks, culverts, dry streambeds, or low-lying ground that appear harmless in dry weather can flood. Every state is at risk from this hazard.

What Would You Do?

You and your family moved from a city neighborhood in San Francisco, California, to a suburb of Phoenix, Arizona. Since earthquakes were a threat in your area, you always kept some extra food, water, and other supplies on hand and maintained an earthquake insurance policy, just in case something happened. You think this kind of preparation is no longer necessary based on what your neighbors have told you.

According to them, the biggest threat they face is lack of water caused by the very dry weather. You continue to see public service announcements from the federal government about flood insurance and the need to protect yourself from flood damage. Surely, there would be no need for flood insurance where you live with its bare hills, deep canyons, and dry land.

Are you at risk for flooding, or is this more of a risk to people who live elsewhere? *Yes.*

Is there a need to have a disaster plan and a disaster supplies kit? *Yes.*

Should you consider purchasing flood insurance? *Yes.*

Know the Terms

Familiarize yourself with these terms to help identify a flood hazard.

FLOOD WATCH: Flooding is possible. Tune in to NOAA Weather Radio, commercial radio, or television for information.

FLASH FLOOD WATCH: Flash flooding is possible. Be prepared to move to higher ground; listen to NOAA Weather Radio, commercial radio, or television for information.

FLOOD WARNING: Flooding is occurring or will occur soon; if advised to evacuate, do so immediately.

FLASH FLOOD WARNING: A flash flood is occurring; seek higher ground on foot immediately.

Take Protective Measures

Before a Flood

To prepare for a flood, you should:

- Avoid building in a floodplain unless you elevate and reinforce your home.
- Elevate the furnace, water heater, and electric panel if susceptible to flooding.
- Install "check valves" in sewer traps to prevent floodwater from backing up into the drains of your home.
- Construct barriers (levees, berms, flood walls) to stop floodwater from entering the building.
- Seal walls in basements with waterproofing compounds to avoid seepage.

During a Flood

If a flood is likely in your area, you should:

- Listen to the radio or television for information.
- Be aware that flash flooding can occur. If there is any possibility of a flash flood, move immediately to higher ground. Do not wait for instructions to move.
- Be aware of streams, drainage channels, canyons, and other areas known to flood suddenly. Flash floods can occur in these areas with or without such typical warnings as rain clouds or heavy rain.

If you must prepare to evacuate, you should do the following:

- Secure your home. If you have time, bring in outdoor furniture. Move essential items to an upper floor.

- Turn off utilities at the main switches or valves if instructed to do so. Disconnect electrical appliances. Do not touch electrical equipment if you are wet or standing in water.

If you have to leave your home, remember these evacuation tips:

- Do not walk through moving water. Six inches of moving water can make you fall. If you have to walk in water, walk where the water is not moving. Use a stick to check the firmness of the ground in front of you.
- Do not drive into flooded areas. If floodwaters rise around your car, abandon the car and move to higher ground if you can do so safely. You and the vehicle can be quickly swept away.

After a Flood

The following are guidelines for the period following a flood:

- Listen for news reports to learn whether the community's water supply is safe to drink.
- Avoid floodwaters; water may be contaminated by oil, gasoline, or raw sewage. Water may also be electrically charged from underground or downed power lines.
- Avoid moving water.
- Be aware of areas where floodwaters have receded. Roads may have weakened and could collapse under the weight of a car.
- Stay away from downed power lines, and report them to the power company.
- Return home only when authorities indicate it is safe.
- Stay out of any building if it is surrounded by floodwaters.

- Use extreme caution when entering buildings; there may be hidden damage, particularly in foundations.
- Service damaged septic tanks, cesspools, pits, and leaching systems as soon as possible. Damaged sewage systems are serious health hazards.
- Clean and disinfect everything that got wet. Mud left from floodwater can contain sewage and chemicals.

The following are important points to remember when driving in flood conditions:

- Six inches of water will reach the bottom of most passenger cars, causing loss of control and possible stalling.
- A foot of water will float many vehicles.
- Two feet of rushing water can carry away most vehicles including sport utility vehicles (SUVs) and pickups.

Additional Information

Flood Insurance

Consider the following facts:

- Flood losses are *not covered* under homeowners' insurance policies.
- FEMA manages the National Flood Insurance Program, which makes federally backed flood insurance available in communities that agree to adopt and enforce floodplain management ordinances to reduce future flood damage.
- Flood insurance is available in most communities through insurance agents.
- There is a thirty-day waiting period before flood insurance goes into effect, so don't delay.
- Flood insurance is available whether the building is in or out of the identified flood-prone area.

KNOWLEDGE CHECK

Decide whether the following statements are true or false. Check the appropriate column. When you have finished, check your answers using the answer key below.

		TRUE	FALSE
1.	Flood emergencies occur in only twelve states.	☐	☐
2.	A "flood watch" announcement on the radio indicates that flooding is possible.	☐	☐
3.	Flash floods may occur with little warning.	☐	☐
4.	Flood risk varies from one region to another.	☐	☐
5.	National flood insurance is available only for buildings within an identified flood-prone area.	☐	☐
6.	It is safe to walk through floodwater if you can see the ground under it.	☐	☐
7.	It takes at least three feet of floodwater to make a motorized vehicle float.	☐	☐
8.	After floodwaters recede from a roadway, the road could still be dangerous.	☐	☐
9.	To prepare for a flood emergency, you should have a NOAA Weather Radio as well as a commercial radio..	☐	☐

Answer key: 1. False; 2. True; 3. True; 4. True; 5. False; 6. False; 7. False; 8. True; 9. True

For More Information

If you require more information about any of these topics, the following are resources that may be helpful.

FEMA Publications

After a Flood: The First Steps. L-198. Information for homeowners on preparedness, safety, and recovery from a flood.

Homeowner's Guide to Retrofitting: Six Ways to Protect Your House from Flooding. L-235. A brochure about obtaining information on how to protect your home from flooding.

Homeowner's Guide to Retrofitting: Six Ways to Protect Your House from Flooding. FEMA-312. A detailed manual on how to protect your home from flooding.

Above the Flood: Elevating Your Floodprone House. FEMA-347. This publication is intended for builders, code officials, and homeowners.

Protecting Building Utilities from Flood Damage. FEMA-348. This publication is intended for developers, architects, engineers, builders, code officials, and homeowners.

Other Publications

AMERICAN RED CROSS

Repairing Your Flooded Home. A sixty-page booklet about how to perform simple home repairs after flooding, including cleaning, sanitation, and determining which professionals to involve for various needed services. Local Red Cross chapters can order in packages of ten as stock number A4477 for a nominal fee. Also available online at www .redcross.org/services/.

NATIONAL WEATHER SERVICE

Hurricane Flooding: A Deadly Inland Danger. 20052. Brochure describing the impact of hurricane flooding and precautions to take. Available online at www.nws.noaa.gov /om/brochures/InlandFlooding.pdf.

The Hidden Danger: Low Water Crossing. 96074E. Brochure describing the hazards of driving your vehicle in flood conditions. Available online at www.nws.noaa.gov/om /brochures/TheHiddenDangerEnglish.pdf.

2.2. TORNADOES

Tornadoes are nature's most violent storms. Spawned from powerful thunderstorms, tornadoes can cause fatalities and devastate a neighborhood in seconds. A tornado appears as a rotating, funnel-shaped cloud that extends from a thunderstorm to the ground with whirling winds that can reach three hundred miles per hour. Damage paths can be in excess of one mile wide and fifty miles long. Every state is at some risk from this hazard.

Some tornadoes are clearly visible, while rain or nearby low-hanging clouds obscure others. Occasionally, tornadoes develop so rapidly that little, if any, advance warning is possible.

Before a tornado hits, the wind may die down and the air may become very still. A cloud of debris can mark the location of a tornado even if a funnel is not visible. Tornadoes generally occur near the trailing edge of a thunderstorm. It is not uncommon to see clear, sunlit skies behind a tornado.

The following are facts about tornadoes:

- They may strike quickly, with little or no warning.
- They may appear nearly transparent until dust and debris are picked up or a cloud forms in the funnel.
- The average tornado moves southwest to northeast, but tornadoes have been known to move in any direction.
- The average forward speed of a tornado is thirty miles per hour, but may vary from stationary to seventy miles per hour.
- Tornadoes can accompany tropical storms and hurricanes as they move onto land.
- Waterspouts are tornadoes that form over water.
- Tornadoes are most frequently reported east of the Rocky Mountains during spring and summer months.
- Peak tornado season in the southern states is March through May; in the northern states, it is late spring through early summer.

- Tornadoes are most likely to occur between 3:00 P.M. and 9:00 P.M., but can occur at any time.

Know the Terms

Familiarize yourself with these terms to help identify a tornado hazard.

TORNADO WATCH: Tornadoes are possible. Remain alert for approaching storms. Watch the sky and stay tuned to NOAA Weather Radio, commercial radio, or television for information.

TORNADO WARNING: A tornado has been sighted or indicated by weather radar. Take shelter immediately.

Take Protective Measures

Be alert to changing weather conditions.

Before a Tornado

- Listen to NOAA Weather Radio or to commercial radio or television newscasts for the latest information.
- Look for approaching storms.
- Look for the following danger signs:
    —Dark, often greenish sky
    —Large hail
    —A large, dark, low-lying cloud (particularly if rotating)
    —Loud roar, similar to a freight train

If you see approaching storms or any of the danger signs, be prepared to take shelter immediately.

During a Tornado

If you are under a tornado warning, seek shelter immediately! If you are in:

A STRUCTURE (E.G. RESIDENCE, SMALL BUILDING, SCHOOL, NURSING HOME, HOSPITAL, FACTORY, SHOPPING CENTER, HIGH-RISE BUILDING)

- Go to a predesignated shelter area such as a safe room, basement, storm cellar, or the lowest building level.
- If there is no basement, go to the center of an interior room on the lowest level (closet, interior hallway) away from corners, windows, doors, and outside walls. Put as many walls as possible between you and the outside. Get under a sturdy table and use your arms to protect your head and neck.
- Do not open windows.

A VEHICLE, TRAILER, OR MOBILE HOME

- Get out immediately and go to the lowest floor of a sturdy, nearby building or a storm shelter. Mobile homes, even if tied down, offer little protection from tornadoes.

THE OUTSIDE WITH NO SHELTER

- Lie flat in a nearby ditch or depression and cover your head with your hands. Be aware of the potential for flooding.
- Do not get under an overpass or bridge. You are safer in a low, flat location.
- Never try to outrun a tornado in urban or congested areas in a car or truck. Instead, leave the vehicle immediately for safe shelter.
- Watch out for flying debris. Flying debris from tornadoes causes most fatalities and injuries.

After a Tornado

Follow the instructions for recovering from a disaster in Part 5.

Preparing a Safe Room

Extreme windstorms in many parts of the country pose a serious threat to buildings and their occupants. Your residence may be built "to code," but that does not mean it can withstand winds from extreme events such as tornadoes and major hurricanes. The purpose of a safe room or a wind shelter is to provide a space where you and your family can seek refuge that provides a high level of protection. You can build a safe room in one of several places in your home:

- Your basement.
- Atop a concrete slab-on-grade foundation or garage floor.
- An interior room on the first floor.

Safe rooms built below ground level provide the greatest protection, but a safe room built in a first-floor interior room also can provide the necessary protection. Below-ground safe rooms must be designed to avoid accumulating water during the heavy rains that often accompany severe windstorms.

To protect its occupants, a safe room must be built to withstand high winds and flying debris, even if the rest of the residence is severely damaged or destroyed. Consider the following when building a safe room:

- The safe room must be adequately anchored to resist overturning and uplift.
- The walls, ceiling, and door of the shelter must withstand wind pressure and resist penetration by windborne objects and falling debris.
- The connections between all parts of the safe room must be strong enough to resist the wind.

- Sections of either interior or exterior residence walls that are used as walls of the safe room must be separated from the structure of the residence so that damage to the residence will not cause damage to the safe room.

FEMA Publications

Taking Shelter from the Storm: Building a Safe Room Inside Your House. L-233. Brochure providing details on obtaining information about how to build a wind-safe room to withstand tornado, hurricane, and other high winds.

Taking Shelter from the Storm: Building a Safe Room Inside Your House. FEMA-320. Manual with detailed information about how to build a wind-safe room to withstand tornado, hurricane, and other high winds.

Locate the Safest Place

Locate the safest place to seek shelter should you not be able to evacuate:

Apartment: Bathroom.

One-story house: Walk-in closet.

Two-story house: First-floor bathroom.

For More Information

If you require more information about any of these topics, the following are resources that may be helpful.

FEMA Publications

Tornado Fact Sheet. L-148. Provides safety tips for before, during, and after a tornado.

Tornado Protection—Selecting Refuge Areas in Buildings.
FEMA 431. Intended primarily to help building adminis-
trators, architects, and engineers select the best available
refuge areas in existing schools.

2.3. HURRICANES

A hurricane is a type of tropical cyclone, the generic term for a
low-pressure system that generally forms in the tropics. A typical cyclone is accompanied by thunderstorms, and in the northern hemisphere, a counterclockwise circulation of winds near
the earth's surface.

All Atlantic and Gulf of Mexico coastal areas are subject to
hurricanes or tropical storms. Parts of the southwestern United
States and the Pacific coast experience heavy rains and floods
each year from hurricanes spawned off Mexico. The Atlantic
hurricane season lasts from June to November, with the peak
season from mid-August to late October.

Hurricanes can cause catastrophic damage to coastlines and
several hundred miles inland. Winds can exceed 155 miles per
hour. Hurricanes and tropical storms can also spawn tornadoes
and microbursts, create storm surges along the coast, and cause
extensive damage from heavy rainfall.

Hurricanes are classified into five categories based on their
wind speed, central pressure, and damage potential (see chart).
Category three and higher hurricanes are considered major hurricanes, though categories one and two are still extremely dangerous and warrant your full attention.

Hurricanes can produce widespread torrential rains. Floods
are the deadly and destructive result. Slow-moving storms and
tropical storms moving into mountainous regions tend to produce especially heavy rain. Excessive rain can trigger landslides
or mud slides, especially in mountainous regions. Flash flooding
can occur due to intense rainfall. Flooding on rivers and streams
may persist for several days or more after the storm.

SAFFIR-SIMPSON HURRICANE SCALE

SCALE NO. (CATEGORY)	SUSTAINED WINDS (MPH)	DAMAGE	STORM SURGE
1	74–95	Minimal: Unanchored mobile homes, vegetation, and signs	4–5 feet
2	96–110	Moderate: All mobile homes, roofs, small craft; flooding	6–8 feet
3	111–130	Extensive: Small buildings; low-lying roads cut off	9–12 feet
4	131–155	Extreme: Roofs destroyed, trees down, roads cut off, mobile homes destroyed, beach homes flooded	13–18 feet
5	Over 155	Catastrophic: Most buildings destroyed, vegetation destroyed, major roads cut off, homes flooded	Greater than 18 feet

Between 1970 and 1999, more people lost their lives from freshwater inland flooding associated with land-falling tropical cyclones than from any other weather hazard related to tropical cyclones.

Naming the Hurricane

Since 1953, Atlantic tropical storms have been named from lists originated by the National Hurricane Center and now maintained and updated by an international committee of the World Meteorological Organization. The lists featured only women's names until 1979. After that, men's and women's names were alternated. Six lists are used in rotation. Thus, the 2012 list will be used again in 2018.

The only time there is a change in the list is if a storm is so deadly or costly that the continued use of the name would be inappropriate for reasons of sensitivity. When this occurs, the name is stricken from the list and another name is selected to replace it.

Sometimes names are changed. Lorenzo replaced Luis and Michelle replaced Marilyn. The complete lists can be found at www.nhc.noaa.gov under "Storm Names."

Know the Terms

Familiarize yourself with these terms to help identify a hurricane hazard.

TROPICAL DEPRESSION: An organized system of clouds and thunderstorms with a defined surface circulation and maximum sustained winds of thirty-eight miles per hour (thirty-three knots) or less. Sustained winds are defined as one-minute-average wind measured at about thirty-three feet (ten meters) above the surface.

TROPICAL STORM: An organized system of strong thunderstorms with a defined surface circulation and maximum sustained winds of thirty-nine to seventy-three miles per hour (thirty-four to sixty-three knots).

HURRICANE: An intense tropical weather system of strong thunderstorms with a well-defined surface circulation and maximum sustained winds of seventy-four miles per hour (sixty-four knots) or higher.

STORM SURGE: A dome of water pushed onshore by hurricane and tropical storm winds. Storm surges can reach twenty-five-feet high and be fifty to one hundred miles wide.

STORM TIDE: A combination of a storm surge and the normal tide (i.e., a fifteen-foot storm surge combined with a two-foot normal high tide over the mean sea level creates a seventeen-foot storm tide).

HURRICANE/TROPICAL STORM WATCH: Hurricane/tropical storm conditions are possible in the specified area, usually within thirty-six hours. Tune in to NOAA Weather Radio, commercial radio, or television for information.

HURRICANE/TROPICAL STORM WARNING: Hurricane/tropical storm conditions are expected in the specified area, usually within twenty-four hours.

SHORT-TERM WATCHES AND WARNINGS: These warnings provide detailed information about specific hurricane threats, such as flash floods and tornadoes.

Take Protective Measures

To prepare for a hurricane, you should take the following measures:

Before a Hurricane

- Make plans to secure your property. Permanent storm shutters offer the best protection for windows. A second option is to board up windows with five-eighth-inch marine plywood, cut to fit and ready to install. Tape does not prevent windows from breaking.
- Install straps or additional clips to securely fasten your roof to the frame structure. This will reduce roof damage.

- Be sure trees and shrubs around your home are well-trimmed.
- Clear loose and clogged rain gutters and downspouts.
- Determine how and where to secure your boat.
- Consider building a safe room.

Review

For more information on safe rooms see section 2.2, Tornadoes.

During a Hurricane

If a hurricane is likely in your area, you should:

- Listen to the radio or TV for information.
- Secure your home, close storm shutters, and secure outdoor objects or bring them indoors.
- Turn off utilities if instructed to do so. Otherwise, turn the refrigerator thermostat to its coldest setting and keep its doors closed.
- Turn off propane tanks.
- Avoid using the phone, except for serious emergencies.
- Moor your boat if time permits.
- Ensure a supply of water for sanitary purposes such as cleaning and flushing toilets. Fill the bathtub and other large containers with water.

You should evacuate under the following conditions:

- If you are directed by local authorities to do so. Be sure to follow their instructions.
- If you live in a mobile home or temporary structure—such shelters are particularly hazardous during hurricanes no matter how well fastened to the ground.
- If you live in a high-rise building—hurricane winds are stronger at higher elevations.

- If you live on the coast, on a floodplain, near a river, or on an inland waterway.
- If you feel you are in danger.

If you are unable to evacuate, go to your wind-safe room. If you do not have one, follow these guidelines:

- Stay indoors during the hurricane and away from windows and glass doors.
- Close all interior doors—secure and brace external doors.
- Keep curtains and blinds closed. Do not be fooled if there is a lull; it could be the eye of the storm—winds will pick up again.
- Take refuge in a small interior room, closet, or hallway on the lowest level.
- Lie on the floor under a table or another sturdy object.

After a Hurricane

Follow the instructions for recovering from a disaster in Part 5.

Review

Guidelines for sheltering, see section 1.4, Shelter.

For More Information

If you require more information about any of these topics, the following are resources that may be helpful:

FEMA Publications

Against the Wind: Protecting Your Home from Hurricane and Wind Damage. FEMA-247. A guide to hurricane preparedness. Available online at www.fema.gov/.

KNOWLEDGE CHECK: YOU MAKE THE CALL

Read the following and respond to the question below. See the answer key below to check your answer.

Your neighbor said that in the event a hurricane threatens, the household would get ready by closing the windows and doors on the storm side of the house and opening the ones on the side away from the wind. They also will tape the windows to prevent damage to the glass. Is this a good idea?

Answer key: No! All of the doors and windows should be closed (and shuttered) throughout the duration of the hurricane. The winds in a hurricane are highly turbulent and any open window or door can be an open target for flying debris.

As for the tape, it is a waste of effort, time, and tape. It offers no strength to the glass and no protection against flying debris.

Community Hurricane Preparedness. IS-324. CD-ROM or Web-based training course for federal, state, and local emergency managers. Web-based version available online at http://meted.ucar.edu/hurrican/chp/index.htm.

Safety Tips for Hurricanes. L 105. Publication for teachers and parents for presentation to children. To order, call (800) 480-2520.

Other Publications

- *Protect Your Home against Hurricane Damage, Institute for Business and Home Safety.* 110 William Street, New York, NY 20038.

2.4. THUNDERSTORMS AND LIGHTNING

All thunderstorms are dangerous. Every thunderstorm produces lightning. In the United States, an average of three hundred people are injured and eighty people are killed each year by lightning. Although most lightning victims survive, people struck by lightning often report a variety of long-term, debilitating symptoms.

Other associated dangers of thunderstorms include tornadoes, strong winds, hail, and flash flooding. Flash flooding is responsible for more fatalities—more than one hundred forty annually—than any other thunderstorm-associated hazard.

Dry thunderstorms that do not produce rain that reaches the ground are most prevalent in the western United States. Falling raindrops evaporate, but lightning can still reach the ground and can start wildfires.

The following are facts about thunderstorms:

- They may occur singly, in clusters, or in lines.
- Some of the most severe occur when a single thunderstorm affects one location for an extended time.
- Thunderstorms typically produce heavy rain for a brief period, anywhere from thirty minutes to an hour.
- Warm, humid conditions are highly favorable for thunderstorm development.
- About 10 percent of thunderstorms are classified as severe— one that produces hail at least three-quarters of an inch in diameter, has winds of fifty-eight miles per hour or higher, or produces a tornado.

The following are facts about lightning:

- Lightning's unpredictability increases the risk to individuals and property.
- Lightning often strikes outside of heavy rain and may occur as far as ten miles away from any rainfall.
- "Heat lightning" is actually lightning from a thunderstorm too far away for thunder to be heard. However, the storm may be moving in your direction!

- Most lightning deaths and injuries occur when people are caught outdoors in the summer months during the afternoon and evening.
- Your chances of being struck by lightning are estimated to be one in six hundred thousand, but could be reduced even further by following safety precautions.
- Lightning strike victims carry no electrical charge and should be attended to immediately.

Know the Terms

Familiarize yourself with these terms to help identify a thunderstorm hazard.

SEVERE THUNDERSTORM WATCH: Tells you when and where severe thunderstorms are likely to occur. Watch the sky and stay tuned to NOAA Weather Radio, commercial radio, or television for information.

SEVERE THUNDERSTORM WARNING: Issued when severe weather has been reported by spotters or indicated by radar. Warnings indicate imminent danger to life and property to those in the path of the storm.

Take Protective Measures

Before Thunderstorms and Lightning

To prepare for a thunderstorm, you should do the following:

- Remove dead or rotting trees and branches that could fall and cause injury or damage during a severe thunderstorm.
- Remember the thirty/thirty lightning safety rule: Go indoors if, after seeing lightning, you cannot count to thirty before hearing thunder. Stay indoors for thirty minutes after hearing the last clap of thunder.

The following are guidelines for what you should do if a thunderstorm is likely in your area:

- Postpone outdoor activities.
- Get inside a home, building, or hard-top automobile (not a convertible). Although you may be injured if lightning strikes your car, you are much safer inside a vehicle than outside.
- Remember, rubber-soled shoes and rubber tires provide *no* protection from lightning. However, the steel frame of a hard-topped vehicle provides increased protection if you are not touching metal.
- Secure outdoor objects that could blow away or cause damage.
- Shutter windows and secure outside doors. If shutters are not available, close window blinds, shades, or curtains.
- Avoid showering or bathing. Plumbing and bathroom fixtures can conduct electricity.
- Use a corded telephone only for emergencies. Cordless and cellular telephones are safe to use.
- Unplug appliances and other electrical items such as computers and turn off air conditioners. Power surges from lightning can cause serious damage.
- Use your battery-operated NOAA Weather Radio for updates from local officials.

Avoid the following:

- Natural lightning rods such as a tall, isolated tree in an open area.
- Hilltops, open fields, the beach, or a boat on the water.
- Isolated sheds or other small structures in open areas.
- Anything metal—tractors, farm equipment, motorcycles, golf carts, golf clubs, and bicycles.

During a Thunderstorm

If you are:

In a forest: Seek shelter in a low area under a thick growth of small trees.

In an open area: Go to a low place such as a ravine or valley. Be alert for flash floods.

On open water: Get to land and find shelter immediately.

Anywhere you feel your hair stand on end (which indicates that lightning is about to strike): Squat low to the ground on the balls of your feet. Place your hands over your ears and your head between your knees. Make yourself the smallest target possible and minimize your contact with the ground. *Do not* lie flat on the ground.

After a Thunderstorm

Call 9-1-1 for medical assistance as soon as possible. The following are things you should check when you attempt to give aid to a victim of lightning:

- Breathing—If breathing has stopped, begin mouth-to-mouth resuscitation.
- Heartbeat—If the heart has stopped, administer CPR.
- Pulse—If the victim has a pulse and is breathing, look for other possible injuries. Check for burns where the lightning entered and left the body. Also be alert for nervous system damage, broken bones, and loss of hearing and eyesight.

For More Information

If you require more information about any of these topics, the following resource may be helpful.

KNOWLEDGE CHECK

Decide whether the following statements are true or false. When you have finished, verify your answers using the answer key below.

1. Every thunderstorm produces lightning.
2. Never touch a person struck by lightning.
3. Dry, cold conditions favor development of a thunderstorm.
4. If you can count to twenty-five after seeing lightning and before hearing thunder, it is safe to stay outdoors.
5. It is safe to use a cordless telephone during a thunderstorm.
6. Rubber-soled shoes and rubber tires provide protection from lightning.

Answer key: 1. True; 2. False; 3. False; 4. False; 5. True; 6. False

National Weather Service Publication

Facts about Lightning. 200252. Two-page fact sheet for boaters. Available online at www.nws.noaa.gov/.

2.5. WINTER STORMS AND EXTREME COLD

Heavy snowfall and extreme cold can immobilize an entire region. Even areas that normally experience mild winters can be hit with a major snowstorm or extreme cold. Winter storms can result in flooding, storm surge, closed highways, blocked roads, downed power lines, and hypothermia.

Know the Terms

Familiarize yourself with these terms to help identify a winter storm hazard.

FREEZING RAIN: Rain that freezes when it hits the ground, creating a coating of ice on roads, walkways, trees, and power lines.

SLEET: Rain that turns to ice pellets before reaching the ground. Sleet also causes moisture on roads to freeze and become slippery.

WINTER STORM WATCH: A winter storm is possible in your area. Tune in to NOAA Weather Radio, commercial radio, or television for more information.

WINTER STORM WARNING: A winter storm is occurring or will soon occur in your area.

BLIZZARD WARNING: Sustained winds or frequent gusts to thirty-five miles per hour or greater and considerable amounts of falling or blowing snow (reducing visibility to less than a quarter mile) are expected to prevail for a period of three hours or longer.

FROST/FREEZE WARNING: Below freezing temperatures are expected.

Take Protective Measures

Before Winter Storms and Extreme Cold

Include the following in your disaster supplies kit:

- Rock salt to melt ice on walkways.
- Sand to improve traction.
- Snow shovels and other snow removal equipment.

Prepare for possible isolation in your home by having sufficient heating fuel; regular fuel sources may be cut off. For example, store a good supply of dry, seasoned wood for your fireplace or wood-burning stove.

Review

See section 1.3, Assemble a Disaster Supplies Kit.

Winterize your home to extend the life of your fuel supply by insulating walls and attics, caulking and weather-stripping doors and windows, and installing storm windows or covering windows with plastic.

To winterize your car, attend to the following:

- Battery and ignition system should be in top condition and battery terminals clean.
- Ensure antifreeze levels are sufficient to avoid freezing.
- Ensure the heater and defroster work properly.
- Check and repair windshield wiper equipment; ensure proper washer fluid level.
- Ensure the thermostat works properly.
- Check lights and flashing hazard lights for serviceability.
- Check for leaks and crimped pipes in the exhaust system; repair or replace as necessary. Carbon monoxide is deadly and usually gives no warning.
- Check brakes for wear and fluid levels.
- Check oil for level and weight. Heavier oils congeal more at low temperatures and do not lubricate as well.
- Consider snow tires, snow tires with studs, or chains.
- Replace fuel and air filters. Keep water out of the system by using additives and maintaining a full tank of gas.

During a Winter Storm

The following are guidelines for what you should do during a winter storm or under conditions of extreme cold:

- Listen to your radio, television, or NOAA Weather Radio for weather reports and emergency information.

- Eat regularly and drink ample fluids, but avoid caffeine and alcohol.
- Avoid overexertion when shoveling snow. Overexertion can bring on a heart attack—a major cause of death in the winter. If you must shovel snow, stretch before going outside.
- Watch for signs of frostbite. These include loss of feeling and white or pale appearance in extremities such as fingers, toes, earlobes, and the tip of the nose. If symptoms are detected, get medical help immediately.
- Watch for signs of hypothermia. These include uncontrollable shivering, memory loss, disorientation, incoherence, slurred speech, drowsiness, and apparent exhaustion. If symptoms of hypothermia are detected, get the victim to a warm location, remove wet clothing, warm the center of the body first, and give warm, nonalcoholic beverages if the victim is conscious. Get medical help as soon as possible.
- Conserve fuel, if necessary, by keeping your residence cooler than normal. Temporarily close off heat to some rooms.
- Maintain ventilation when using kerosene heaters to avoid build-up of toxic fumes. Refuel kerosene heaters outside and keep them at least three feet from flammable objects.

DRESS FOR THE WEATHER

- Wear several layers of loose fitting, lightweight, warm clothing rather than one layer of heavy clothing. The outer garments should be tightly woven and water repellent.
- Wear mittens, which are warmer than gloves.
- Wear a hat.
- Cover your mouth with a scarf to protect your lungs.
- Drive only if it is absolutely necessary. If you must drive, consider the following:

    —Travel in the day, don't travel alone, and keep others informed of your schedule.

    —Stay on main roads; avoid back road shortcuts.

If a blizzard traps you in the car, keep these guidelines in mind:

- Pull off the highway. Turn on hazard lights and hang a distress flag from the radio antenna or window.
- Remain in your vehicle, where rescuers are most likely to find you. Do not set out on foot unless you can see a building close by where you know you can take shelter. Be careful; distances are distorted by blowing snow. A building may seem close, but be too far to walk to in deep snow.
- Run the engine and heater about ten minutes each hour to keep warm. When the engine is running, open an upwind window slightly for ventilation. This will protect you from possible carbon monoxide poisoning. Periodically clear snow from the exhaust pipe.
- Exercise to maintain body heat, but avoid overexertion. In extreme cold, use road maps, seat covers, and floor mats for insulation. Huddle with passengers and use your coat for a blanket.
- Take turns sleeping. One person should be awake at all times to look for rescue crews.
- Drink fluids to avoid dehydration.
- Be careful not to waste battery power. Balance electrical energy needs—the use of lights, heat, and radio—with supply.
- Turn on the inside light at night so work crews or rescuers can see you.
- If stranded in a remote area, stomp large block letters in an open area spelling out HELP or SOS and line with rocks or tree limbs to attract the attention of rescue personnel who may be surveying the area by airplane.
- Leave the car and proceed on foot—if necessary—once the blizzard passes.

After a Winter Storm

Follow the instructions for recovering from a disaster in Part 5.

For More Information

If you require more information about any of these topics, the following are resources that may be helpful:

National Weather Service Publication

Winter Storms . . . The Deceptive Killers. Brochure packed with useful information including winter storm facts, how to detect frostbite and hypothermia, what to do in a winter storm, and how to be prepared. Available online at www .nws.noaa.gov/om/brochures/wntrstm.htm.

Centers for Disease Control and Prevention Publication

Extreme Cold: A Prevention Guide to Promote Your Personal Health and Safety. An extensive document providing information about planning ahead for cold weather, safety both indoors and outdoors in cold weather, and cold weather health conditions. Available online at www .cdc.gov.

2.6. EXTREME HEAT

Heat kills by pushing the human body beyond its limits. In extreme heat and high humidity, evaporation is slowed and the body must work extra hard to maintain a normal temperature.

Most heat disorders occur because the victim has been overexposed to heat or has overexercised for his or her age and physical condition. Older adults, young children, and those who are sick or overweight are more likely to succumb to extreme heat.

Conditions that can induce heat-related illnesses include stagnant atmospheric conditions and poor air quality. Consequently, people living in urban areas may be at greater risk from the effects of a prolonged heat wave than those living in rural areas. Also, asphalt and concrete store heat longer and gradually release heat at night, which can produce higher nighttime temperatures known as the "urban heat island effect."

Know the Terms

Familiarize yourself with these terms to help identify an extreme heat hazard.

HEAT WAVE: Prolonged period of excessive heat, often combined with excessive humidity.

HEAT INDEX: A number in degrees Fahrenheit (F) that tells how hot it feels when relative humidity is added to the air temperature. Exposure to full sunshine can increase the heat index by fifteen degrees.

HEAT CRAMPS: Muscular pains and spasms due to heavy exertion. Although heat cramps are the least severe, they are often the first signal that the body is having trouble with the heat.

HEAT EXHAUSTION: Typically occurs when people exercise heavily or work in a hot, humid place where body fluids are lost through heavy sweating. Blood flow to the skin increases, causing blood flow to decrease to the vital organs. This results in a form of mild shock. If not treated, the victim's condition will worsen. Body temperature will keep rising and the victim may suffer heat stroke.

HEAT STROKE: A life-threatening condition. The victim's temperature control system, which produces sweating to cool the body, stops working. The body temperature can rise so high that brain damage and death may result if the body is not cooled quickly.

SUN STROKE: Another term for heat stroke.

Take Protective Measures

Before Extreme Heat

To prepare for extreme heat, you should:

- Install window air conditioners snugly; insulate if necessary.
- Check air-conditioning ducts for proper insulation.
- Install temporary window reflectors (for use between windows and drapes), such as aluminum foil–covered cardboard, to reflect heat back outside.
- Weather-strip doors and sills to keep cool air in.
- Cover windows that receive morning or afternoon sun with drapes, shades, awnings, or louvers. (Outdoor awnings or louvers can reduce the heat that enters a home by up to 80 percent.)
- Keep storm windows up all year.

During a Heat Emergency

The following are guidelines for what you should do if the weather is extremely hot.

- Stay indoors as much as possible and limit exposure to the sun.
- Stay on the lowest floor out of the sunshine if air-conditioning is not available.
- Consider spending the warmest part of the day in public buildings such as libraries, schools, movie theaters, shopping malls, and other community facilities. Circulating air can cool the body by increasing the perspiration rate of evaporation.

- Eat well-balanced, light, and regular meals. Avoid using salt tablets unless directed to do so by a physician.

- Drink plenty of water. Persons who have epilepsy or heart, kidney, or liver disease; are on fluid-restricted diets; or have a problem with fluid retention should consult a doctor before increasing liquid intake.

- Limit intake of alcoholic beverages.

- Dress in loose-fitting, lightweight, and light-colored clothes that cover as much skin as possible.

- Protect face and head by wearing a wide-brimmed hat.

- Check on family, friends, and neighbors who do not have air-conditioning and who spend much of their time alone.

- Never leave children or pets alone in closed vehicles.

- Avoid strenuous work during the warmest part of the day. Use a buddy system when working in extreme heat, and take frequent breaks.

FIRST AID FOR HEAT-INDUCED ILLNESSES

Extreme heat brings with it the possibility of heat-induced illnesses. The following lists these illnesses, their symptoms, and the first-aid treatment.

CONDITION: SUNBURN

Symptoms: Skin redness and pain, possible swelling, blisters, fever, headaches.

First Aid:

- Take a shower using soap to remove oils that may block pores, preventing the body from cooling naturally.
- Apply dry, sterile dressings to any blisters, and get medical attention.

CONDITION: HEAT CRAMPS

Symptoms: Painful spasms, usually in leg and abdominal muscles; heavy sweating.

First Aid:

- Get the victim to a cooler location.
- Lightly stretch and gently massage affected muscles to relieve spasms.
- Give sips of up to a half glass of cool water every fifteen minutes. (Do not give liquids with caffeine or alcohol.)
- Discontinue liquids if victim is nauseated.

CONDITION: HEAT EXHAUSTION

Symptoms: Heavy sweating but skin may be cool, pale, or flushed. Weak pulse. Normal body temperature is possible, but temperature will likely rise. Fainting or dizziness, nausea, vomiting, exhaustion, and headaches are possible.

First Aid:

- Get victim to lie down in a cool place.
- Loosen or remove clothing.
- Apply cool, wet cloths.
- Fan or move victim to air-conditioned place.
- Give sips of water if victim is conscious.
- Be sure water is consumed slowly.
- Give a half glass of cool water every fifteen minutes.
- Discontinue water if victim is nauseated.
- Seek immediate medical attention if vomiting occurs.

CONDITION: HEAT STROKE (A SEVERE MEDICAL EMERGENCY)

Symptoms: High body temperature (105+ degrees); hot, red, dry skin; rapid, weak pulse; and rapid, shallow breathing. Victim will probably not sweat unless victim was sweating from recent strenuous activity. Possible unconsciousness.

First Aid:

- Call 9-1-1 or emergency medical services, or get the victim to a hospital immediately. Delay can be fatal.

- Move victim to a cooler environment.
- Remove clothing.
- Try a cool bath, sponging, or wet sheet to reduce body temperature.
- Watch for breathing problems.
- Use extreme caution.
- Use fans and air conditioners.

After Extreme Heat

Follow the instructions for recovering from a disaster in Part 5.

Additional Information

An emergency water shortage can be caused by prolonged drought, poor water supply management, or contamination of a surface water supply source or aquifer.

Drought can affect vast territorial regions and large population numbers. Drought also creates environmental conditions that increase the risk of other hazards such as fire, flash flood, and possible landslides and debris flow.

Conserving water means more water is available for critical needs for everyone. Appendix A contains detailed suggestions for conserving water both indoors and outdoors. Make these practices a part of your daily life and help preserve this essential resource.

For More Information

If you require more information about any of these topics, the following resource may be helpful.

National Weather Service Publication

Heat Wave: A Major Summer Killer. An online brochure describing the heat index, heat disorders, and heat wave

---

KNOWLEDGE CHECK

You and a friend have been outdoors in the sun for some time. Shortly after coming inside, your friend complains of nausea and a headache but tells you not to worry as it is probably a food allergy. What would you advise him or her to do?

Answer: Seek immediate medical attention and discontinue intake of water.

---

safety tips. Available online at www.nws.noaa.gov/om /brochures/heat_wave.shtml.

2.7. EARTHQUAKES

One of the most frightening and destructive phenomena of nature is a severe earthquake and its terrible aftereffects. An earthquake is a sudden movement of the earth, caused by the abrupt release of strain that has accumulated over a long time. For hundreds of millions of years, the forces of plate tectonics have shaped the earth, as the huge plates that form the earth's surface slowly move over, under, and past each other. Sometimes, the movement is gradual. At other times, the plates are locked together, unable to release the accumulating energy. When the accumulated energy grows strong enough, the plates break free. If the earthquake occurs in a populated area, it may cause many deaths and injuries and extensive property damage.

Know the Terms

Familiarize yourself with these terms to help identify an earthquake hazard.

EARTHQUAKE: A sudden slipping or movement of a portion of the earth's crust, accompanied and followed by a series of vibrations.

AFTERSHOCK: An earthquake of similar or lesser intensity that follows the main earthquake.

FAULT: The fracture across which displacement has occurred during an earthquake. The slippage may range from less than an inch to more than ten yards in a severe earthquake.

EPICENTER: The place on the earth's surface directly above the point on the fault where the earthquake rupture began. Once fault slippage begins, it expands along the fault during the earthquake and can extend hundreds of miles before stopping.

SEISMIC WAVES: Vibrations that travel outward from the earthquake fault at speeds of several miles per second. Although fault slippage directly under a structure can cause considerable damage, the vibrations of seismic waves cause most of the destruction during earthquakes.

MAGNITUDE: The amount of energy released during an earthquake, which is computed from the amplitude of the seismic waves. A magnitude of 7.0 on the Richter scale indicates an extremely strong earthquake. Each whole number on the scale represents an increase of about thirty times more energy released than the previous whole number represents. Therefore, an earthquake measuring 6.0 is about thirty times more powerful than one measuring 5.0.

Take Protective Measures

Before an Earthquake

The following are things you can do to protect yourself, your family, and your property in the event of an earthquake:

- Repair defective electrical wiring, leaky gas lines, and inflexible utility connections. Get appropriate professional help. Do not work with gas or electrical lines yourself.

- Bolt down and secure to the wall studs your water heater, refrigerator, furnace, and gas appliances. If recommended by your gas company, have an automatic gas shut-off valve installed that is triggered by strong vibrations.

- Place large or heavy objects on lower shelves. Fasten shelves, mirrors, and large picture frames to walls. Brace high and top-heavy objects.

- Store bottled foods, glass, china, and other breakables on low shelves or in cabinets that fasten shut.

- Anchor overhead lighting fixtures.

- Be sure the residence is firmly anchored to its foundation.

- Install flexible pipe fittings to avoid gas or water leaks. Flexible fittings are more resistant to breakage.

- Locate safe spots in each room under a sturdy table or against an inside wall. Reinforce this information by moving to these places during each drill.

- Hold earthquake drills with your family members: Drop, cover, and hold on!

During an Earthquake

Minimize your movements during an earthquake to a few steps to a nearby safe place. Stay indoors until the shaking has stopped and you are sure exiting is safe.

If you are indoors:

- Take cover under a sturdy desk, table, or bench or against an inside wall, and hold on. If there isn't a table or desk near you, cover your face and head with your arms and crouch in an inside corner of the building.

- Stay away from glass, windows, outside doors and walls, and anything that could fall, such as lighting fixtures or furniture.

- Stay in bed—if you are there when the earthquake strikes, hold on and protect your head with a pillow, unless you are under a heavy light fixture that could fall. In that case, move to the nearest safe place.

- Use a doorway for shelter only if it is in proximity to you and if you know it is a strongly supported, load-bearing doorway.
- Stay inside until the shaking stops and it is safe to go outside. Most injuries during earthquakes occur when people are hit by falling objects when entering into or exiting from buildings.
- Be aware that the electricity may go out or the sprinkler systems or fire alarms may turn on.
- *Do not* use the elevators.

If you are outdoors:

- Stay there.
- Move away from buildings, streetlights, and utility wires.

If you are in a moving vehicle:

- Stop as quickly as safety permits and stay in the vehicle. Avoid stopping near or under buildings, trees, overpasses, and utility wires.
- Proceed cautiously once the earthquake has stopped, watching for road and bridge damage.

If you are trapped under debris:

- Do not light a match.
- Do not move about or kick up dust.
- Cover your mouth with a handkerchief or clothing.
- Tap on a pipe or wall so rescuers can locate you. Use a whistle if one is available. Shout only as a last resort—shouting can cause you to inhale dangerous amounts of dust.

After an Earthquake

- Be prepared for aftershocks. These secondary shockwaves are usually less violent than the main quake but can be strong enough to do additional damage to weakened structures.
- Open cabinets cautiously. Beware of objects that can fall off shelves.
- Stay away from damaged areas unless your assistance has been specifically requested by police, fire, or relief organizations.
- Be aware of possible tsunamis if you live in coastal areas. These are also known as seismic sea waves (mistakenly called "tidal waves"). When local authorities issue a tsunami warning, assume that a series of dangerous waves is on the way. Stay away from the beach.

For More Information

If you require more information about any of these topics, the following are resources that may be helpful.

FEMA Publications

Avoiding Earthquake Damage: A Checklist for Homeowners. Safety tips for before, during, and after an earthquake.

Preparedness in High-Rise Buildings. FEMA-76. Earthquake safety tips for high-rise dwellers.

Learning to Live in Earthquake Country: Preparedness in Apartments and Mobile Homes. L-143. Safety tips on earthquake preparation for residents of apartments and mobile homes.

Family Earthquake Safety Home Hazard Hunt and Drill. FEMA-113. How to identify home hazards; how to conduct earthquake drills.

KNOWLEDGE CHECK

Check your knowledge about what to do during an earthquake. For each question, choose answer A or B and circle the correct response. When you have finished, check your responses using the answer key below.

What action should you take during an earthquake? The answer varies by where you are when an earthquake strikes. For each situation, pick the best course of action from the choices given.

1. At home
   a. Stay inside.
   b. Go out to the street.

2. In bed
   a. Stand by a window to see what is happening.
   b. Stay in bed and protect your head with a pillow.

3. In any building
   a. Stand in a doorway.
   b. Crouch in an inside corner away from the exterior wall.

4. On the upper floor of an apartment building
   a. Take the elevator to the ground floor as quickly as possible.
   b. Stay in an interior room under a desk or table.

5. Outdoors
   a. Run into the nearest building.
   b. Stay outside away from buildings.

6. Driving a car
   a. Stop the car in an open area.
   b. Stop the car under an overpass.

Answer key: 1. a; 2. b; 3. b; 4. b; 5. b; 6. a

Earthquake Preparedness: What Every Childcare Provider Should Know. FEMA 240. Publication for teachers and for presentation to children. Available online at www.fema .gov/kids/tch_eq.htm.

2.8. VOLCANOES

A volcano is a vent through which molten rock escapes to the earth's surface. When pressure from gases within the molten rock becomes too great, an eruption occurs. Eruptions can be quiet or explosive. There may be lava flows, flattened landscapes, poisonous gases, and flying rock and ash.

Because of their intense heat, lava flows are great fire hazards. Lava flows destroy everything in their path, but most move slowly enough that people can move out of the way.

Fresh volcanic ash, made of pulverized rock, can be abrasive, acidic, gritty, gassy, and odorous. While not immediately dangerous to most adults, the acidic gas and ash can cause lung damage to small infants, to older adults, and to those suffering from severe respiratory illnesses. Volcanic ash also can damage machinery, including engines and electrical equipment. Ash accumulations mixed with water become heavy and can collapse roofs.

Volcanic eruptions can be accompanied by other natural hazards, including earthquakes, mudflows and flash floods, rock falls and landslides, acid rain, fire, and (under special conditions) tsunamis. Active volcanoes in the U.S. are found mainly in Hawaii, Alaska, and the Pacific Northwest.

Take Protective Measures

Before a Volcanic Eruption

- Add a pair of goggles and a disposable breathing mask for each member of the family to your disaster supplies kit.
- Stay away from active volcano sites.

During a Volcanic Eruption

The following are guidelines for what to do if a volcano erupts in your area:

- Evacuate immediately from the volcano area to avoid flying debris, hot gases, lateral blast, and lava flow.
- Be aware of mudflows. The danger from a mudflow increases near stream channels and with prolonged heavy rains. Mudflows can move faster than you can walk or run. Look upstream before crossing a bridge, and do not cross the bridge if mudflow is approaching.
- Avoid river valleys and low-lying areas.

PROTECTION FROM FALLING ASH

- Wear long-sleeved shirts and long pants.
- Use goggles and wear eyeglasses instead of contact lenses.
- Use a dust mask or hold a damp cloth over your face to help with breathing.
- Stay away from areas downwind from the volcano to avoid volcanic ash.
- Stay indoors until the ash has settled unless there is danger of the roof collapsing.
- Close doors, windows, and all ventilation in the house (chimney vents, furnaces, air conditioners, fans, and other vents).
- Clear heavy ash from flat or low-pitched roofs and rain gutters.
- Avoid running car or truck engines. Driving can stir up volcanic ash that can clog engines, damage moving parts, and stall vehicles.
- Avoid driving in heavy ash fall unless absolutely required. If you have to drive, keep speed down to thirty-five miles per hour or slower.

After a Volcanic Eruption

Follow the instructions for recovering from a disaster in Part 5.

> ### KNOWLEDGE CHECK
>
> Read the scenario and answer the question. Check your responses with the answer key below.
>
> About an hour after the eruption of Mount St. Helens, ash began to fall in Yakima, a city in eastern Washington. The ash fall was so extensive and it became so dark that lights were turned on all day. It took ten weeks to haul away the ash from Yakima's streets, sidewalks, and roofs. Assume you were a resident of Yakima during this time. What would you need to protect yourself when going outside?
>
> *Answer key:* 1. Face masks. 2. Goggles. 3. Eyeglasses instead of contact lenses. 4. Clothing to cover as much of the body as possible.

For More Information

If you require more information about any of these topics, the following resource may be helpful.

Volcano Hazards Program. Web site with volcano activity updates, feature stories, information about volcano hazards, and resources. Available online at http://volcanoes.usgs.gov.

2.9. LANDSLIDES AND DEBRIS FLOWS (MUD SLIDES)

Landslides occur in all U.S. states and territories. In a landslide, masses of rock, earth, or debris move down a slope. Landslides may be small or large, slow or rapid. They are activated by storms, earthquakes, volcanic eruptions, fires, and human modification of land.

Debris and mud flows are rivers of rock, earth, and other debris saturated with water. They develop when water rapidly accumulates in the ground, during heavy rainfall or rapid snowmelt, changing the earth into a flowing river of mud or "slurry." They can flow rapidly, striking with little or no warning at avalanche speeds. They also can travel several miles from their source, growing in size as they pick up trees, boulders, cars, and other materials.

Landslide problems can be caused by land mismanagement, particularly in mountain, canyon, and coastal regions. Land-use zoning, professional inspections, and proper design can minimize many landslide, mudflow, and debris flow problems.

Take Protective Measures

Before a Landslide or Debris Flow

The following are steps you can take to protect yourself from the effects of a landslide or debris flow.

- Do not build near steep slopes, close to mountain edges, near drainage ways, or near natural erosion valleys.
- Get a ground assessment of your property.
- Consult an appropriate professional expert for advice on corrective measures.
- Minimize home hazards by having flexible pipe fittings installed to avoid gas or water leaks, as flexible fittings are more resistant to breakage (only the gas company or professionals should install gas fittings).

RECOGNIZE LANDSLIDE WARNING SIGNS

Some warning signs to look for include the following:

- Changes occur in your landscape such as patterns of storm-water drainage on slopes (especially the places where runoff water converges), land movement, small slides, flows, or progressively leaning trees.

- Doors or windows stick or jam for the first time.
- New cracks appear in plaster, tile, brick, or foundations.
- Outside walls, walks, or stairs begin pulling away from the building.
- Slowly developing, widening cracks appear on the ground or on paved areas such as streets or driveways.
- Underground utility lines break.
- Bulging ground appears at the base of a slope.
- Water breaks through the ground surface in new locations.
- Fences, retaining walls, utility poles, or trees tilt or move.
- A faint rumbling sound that increases in volume is noticeable as the landslide nears.
- The ground slopes downward in one direction and may begin shifting in that direction under your feet.
- Unusual sounds, such as trees cracking or boulders knocking together, might indicate moving debris.
- Collapsed pavement, mud, fallen rocks, and other indications of possible debris flow can be seen when driving (embankments along roadsides are particularly susceptible to landslides).

During a Landslide or Debris Flow

The following are guidelines for what you should do if a landslide or debris flow occurs:

- Move away from the path of a landslide or debris flow as quickly as possible.
- Curl into a tight ball and protect your head if escape is not possible.

KNOWLEDGE CHECK

Review the following information and answer the questions. Check your responses with the answer key below.

Landslides occur in all fifty states—it is estimated that they cause between twenty-five and fifty deaths each year in the U.S. and thousands more in vulnerable areas around the globe. The number of landslides in the United States is expected to increase.

1. What might account for the projected increase in landslides?
2. What can you do to help reverse the upward trend?

Answer key:

1. Mounting pressure for approving the development of lands subject to landslides and earth failures has increased development in these unsafe areas.
2. Work with others in the community to enact and enforce regulations that prohibit building near areas subject to landslides and mud slides. In areas where the hazard exists and development has already occurred, work to promote protective measures such as encouraging homeowners to get a professional ground assessment of their property and educating residents about the warning signs.

After a Landslide or Debris Flow

The following are guidelines for the period following a landslide:

- Stay away from the slide area. There may be danger of additional slides.
- Check for injured and trapped persons near the slide, without entering the direct slide area. Direct rescuers to their locations.
- Watch for associated dangers such as broken electrical, water, gas, and sewage lines and damaged roadways and railways.

- Replant damaged ground as soon as possible since erosion caused by loss of ground cover can lead to flash flooding and additional landslides in the near future.
- Seek advice from a geotechnical expert for evaluating landslide hazards or designing corrective techniques to reduce landslide risk.
- Follow the instructions for returning home in Part 5.

2.10. TSUNAMIS

Tsunamis (pronounced soo-*na*-mees), also known as seismic sea waves (mistakenly called "tidal waves"), are a series of enormous waves created by an underwater disturbance such as an earthquake, landslide, volcanic eruption, or meteorite. A tsunami can move hundreds of miles per hour in the open ocean and smash into land with waves as high as one hundred feet or more.

From the area where the tsunami originates, waves travel outward in all directions. Once the wave approaches the shore, it builds in height. The topography of the coastline and the ocean floor will influence the size of the wave. There may be more than one wave and the succeeding one may be larger than the one before. That is why a small tsunami at one beach can be a giant wave a few miles away.

All tsunamis are potentially dangerous, even though they may not damage every coastline they strike. In the United States, a tsunami can strike anywhere along most of the coastlines; the most destructive tsunamis in the country have occurred along the coasts of California, Oregon, Washington, Alaska, and Hawaii.

Earthquake-induced movement of the ocean floor most often generates tsunamis. If a major earthquake or landslide occurs close to shore, the first wave in a series could reach the beach in a few minutes, even before a warning is issued. Areas are at greater risk if they are less than twenty-five feet above sea level and within a mile of the shoreline. Drowning is the most common cause of death associated with a tsunami. Tsunami waves and the receding water are very destructive to structures in the run-up zone. Other hazards include flooding, contamination of drinking water, and fires from gas lines or ruptured tanks.

Know the Terms

Familiarize yourself with these terms to help identify a tsunami hazard.

ADVISORY: An earthquake has occurred in the Pacific basin, which might generate a tsunami.

WATCH: A tsunami was or may have been generated, but is at least two hours travel time to the area in Watch status.

WARNING: A tsunami was, or may have been generated, which could cause damage; therefore, people in the warned area are strongly advised to evacuate.

Take Protective Measures

The following are guidelines for what you should do if a tsunami is likely in your area:

During a Tsunami

- Turn on your radio to learn if there is a tsunami warning if an earthquake occurs and you are in a coastal area.
- Move inland to higher ground immediately and stay there.

Warning: If there is noticeable recession in water away from the shoreline, this is nature's tsunami warning and it should be heeded. You should move away immediately.

After a Tsunami

The following are guidelines for the period following a tsunami:

- Stay away from flooded and damaged areas until officials say it is safe to return.
- Stay away from debris in the water; it may pose a safety hazard to boats and people.

Save Yourself—Not Your Possessions

Like everyone else in Maullin, Chile, Ramon Atala survived the 1960 Chile earthquake. However, he lost his life trying to save something from the tsunami that followed.

Mr. Atala was Maullin's most prosperous merchant. Outside of town, he owned a barn and a plantation of Monterey pine. In town, he owned a pier and at least one large building and also had private quarters in a waterfront warehouse.

Mr. Atala entered this warehouse between the first and second wave of the tsunami that struck Maullin. The warehouse was washed away and his body was never found.

It is unclear what he was trying to save. What is clear is that no possession is worth your life and that it is important to get to higher ground away from the coast and stay there until it is safe to return.

2.11. FIRES

Each year, more than four thousand Americans die and more than twenty-five thousand are injured in fires, many of which could be prevented. Direct property loss due to fires is estimated at $8.6 billion annually.

To protect yourself, it is important to understand the basic characteristics of fire. Fire spreads quickly; there is no time to gather valuables or make a phone call. In just two minutes, a fire can become life-threatening. In five minutes, a residence can be engulfed in flames.

Heat and smoke from fire can be more dangerous than the flames. Inhaling the superhot air can sear your lungs. Fire produces poisonous gases that make you disoriented and drowsy. Instead of being awakened by a fire, you may fall into a deeper sleep. Asphyxiation is the leading cause of fire deaths, exceeding burns by a three-to-one ratio.

Take Protective Measures

Before a Fire

SMOKE ALARMS

- Install smoke alarms. Properly working smoke alarms decrease your chances of dying in a fire by half.
- Place smoke alarms on every level of your residence. Place them outside bedrooms on the ceiling or high on the wall (four to twelve inches from ceiling), at the top of open stairways, or at the bottom of enclosed stairs and near (but not in) the kitchen.
- Test and clean smoke alarms once a month and replace batteries at least once a year. Replace smoke alarms once every ten years.

PLANS FOR ESCAPING THE FIRE

- Review escape routes with your family. Practice escaping from each room.
- Make sure windows are not nailed or painted shut. Make sure security gratings on windows have a fire safety opening feature so they can be easily opened from the inside.
- Consider escape ladders if your residence has more than one level, and ensure that burglar bars and other antitheft

mechanisms that block outside window entry are easily opened from the inside.

- Teach family members to stay low to the floor (where the air is safer in a fire) when escaping from a fire.
- Clean out storage areas. Do not let trash, such as old newspapers and magazines, accumulate.

FLAMMABLE ITEMS

- Never use gasoline, benzine, naphtha, or similar flammable liquids indoors.
- Store flammable liquids in approved containers in well-ventilated storage areas.
- Never smoke near flammable liquids.
- Discard all rags or materials that have been soaked in flammable liquids after you have used them. Safely discard them outdoors in a metal container.
- Insulate chimneys and place spark arresters on top. The chimney should be at least three feet higher than the roof. Remove branches hanging above and around the chimney.

HEATING SOURCES

- Be careful when using alternative heating sources.
- Check with your local fire department on the legality of using kerosene heaters in your community. Be sure to fill kerosene heaters outside, and be sure they have cooled.
- Place heaters at least three feet away from flammable materials. Make sure the floor and nearby walls are properly insulated.
- Use only the type of fuel designated for your unit and follow manufacturer's instructions.
- Store fireplace ashes in a metal container outside and away from your residence.

- Keep open flames away from walls, furniture, drapery, and flammable items.
- Keep a screen in front of the fireplace.
- Have heating units inspected and cleaned annually by a certified specialist.

MATCHES AND SMOKING

- Keep matches and lighters up high, away from children, and, if possible, in a locked cabinet.
- Never smoke in bed or when drowsy or medicated. Provide smokers with deep, sturdy ashtrays. Douse cigarette and cigar butts with water before disposal.

ELECTRICAL WIRING

- Have the electrical wiring in your residence checked by an electrician.
- Inspect extension cords for frayed or exposed wires or loose plugs.
- Make sure outlets have cover plates and no exposed wiring.
- Make sure wiring does not run under rugs, over nails, or across high-traffic areas.
- Do not overload extension cords or outlets. If you need to plug in two or three appliances, get a UL-approved unit with built-in circuit breakers to prevent sparks and short circuits.
- Make sure insulation does not touch bare electrical wiring.

OTHER

- Sleep with your door closed.
- Install ABC-type fire extinguishers in your residence and teach family members how to use them.
- Consider installing an automatic fire sprinkler system in your residence.

- Ask your local fire department to inspect your residence for fire safety and prevention.

During a Fire

If your clothes catch on fire, you should:

- *Stop, drop, and roll*—until the fire is extinguished. Running only makes the fire burn *faster*.

To escape a fire, you should:

- *Check closed doors for heat before you open them.* If you are escaping through a closed door, use the back of your hand to feel the top of the door, the doorknob, and the crack between the door and door frame before you open it. Never use the palm of your hand or fingers to test for heat—burning those areas could impair your ability to escape a fire (i.e., ladders and crawling).

HOT DOOR: Do not open. Escape through a window. If you cannot escape, hang a white or light-colored sheet outside the window, alerting firefighters to your presence.

COOL DOOR: Open slowly and ensure fire and/or smoke is not blocking your escape route. If your escape route is blocked, shut the door immediately and use an alternate escape route, such as a window. If clear, leave immediately through the door and close it behind you. Be prepared to crawl. Smoke and heat rise. The air is clearer and cooler near the floor.

- Crawl low under any smoke to your exit—heavy smoke and poisonous gases collect first along the ceiling.
- Close doors behind you as you escape to delay the spread of the fire.
- Stay out once you are safely out. Do not reenter. Call 9-1-1.

After a Fire

The following are guidelines for different circumstances in the period following a fire.

- If you are with burn victims, or are a burn victim yourself, call 9-1-1; cool and cover burns to reduce the chance of further injury or infection.
- If you detect heat or smoke when entering a damaged building, evacuate immediately.
- If you are a tenant, contact the landlord.
- If you have a safe or strong box, do not try to open it. It can hold intense heat for several hours. If the door is opened before the box has cooled, the contents could burst into flames.
- If you must leave your home because a building inspector says the building is unsafe, ask someone you trust to watch the property during your absence.
- Follow the instructions for recovering from a disaster in Part 5.

For More Information

If you require more information about any of these topics, the following are resources that may be helpful.

FEMA Publications

After the Fire: Returning to Normal. FA 046. This sixteen-page booklet provides information about recovering from a fire, including what to do during the first twenty-four hours, insurance considerations, valuing your property, replacement of valuable documents, salvage hints, fire department operations, and more. Available online at www.usfa.fema.gov/.

KNOWLEDGE CHECK

Answer each question and check your responses using the answer key below.

1. You need to escape a fire through a closed door. What, if anything, should you do before opening the door?
2. What should you do if your clothes are on fire?
3. What actions should be taken for burn victims?
4. To reduce heating costs, you installed a wood-burning stove. What can you do to reduce the risk of fire from this heating source?
5. To escape in thick smoke, what should you do?

Answer key:

1. Check the door for heat with the back of your hand.
2. Stop, drop, and roll.
3. Call 9-1-1 and cool and cover burns.
4. Have the stove cleaned and inspected by a certified specialist.
5. Crawl close to the floor.

Protecting Your Family from Fire. FA 130. This pamphlet was written to provide the information you need to decide what you must do to protect your family from fire. Topics include children, sleepwear, older adults, smoke detectors, escape plans, and residential sprinklers. Available online at www.usfa.fema.gov/.

Fire Risks for the Hard of Hearing. FA 202. *Fire Risks for the Older Adult.* FA 203. *Fire Risks for the Mobility Impaired.* FA 204. *Fire Risks for the Blind or Visually Impaired.* FA 205. These reports address preparation for fire risks for populations with special challenges. Available online at www.usfa.fema.gov/fire-service/education/education-pubs.shtm.

2.12. WILDFIRES

If you live on a remote hillside or in a valley, prairie, or forest where flammable vegetation is abundant, your residence could be vulnerable to wildfires. These fires are usually triggered by lightning or accidents. Wildfires spread quickly, igniting brush, trees, and homes.

Take Protective Measures

Before a Wildfire

To prepare for wildfires, you should do the following:

- Mark the entrance to your property with address signs that are clearly visible from the road.
- Keep lawns trimmed, leaves raked, and the roof and rain gutters free from debris such as dead limbs and leaves.
- Stack firewood at least thirty feet away from your residence.
- Store flammable materials, liquids, and solvents in metal containers outside your residence at least thirty feet away from structures and wooden fences.
- Create defensible space by thinning trees and brush within thirty feet around your residence. Beyond thirty feet, remove dead wood, debris, and low tree branches.
- Landscape your property with fire-resistant plants and vegetation to prevent fire from spreading quickly. For example, hardwood trees are more fire-resistant than pine, evergreen, eucalyptus, or fir trees.
- Make sure water sources, such as hydrants, ponds, swimming pools, and wells, are accessible to the fire department.
- Use fire-resistant, protective roofing and materials like stone, brick, and metal to protect your residence. Avoid using wood materials. They offer the least fire protection.

- Cover all exterior vents, attic vents, and eaves with metal mesh screens no larger than six millimeters or one-quarter inch to prevent debris from collecting and to help keep sparks out.
- Install multipane windows, tempered safety glass, or fireproof shutters to protect large windows from radiant heat.
- Use fire-resistant draperies for added window protection.
- Have chimneys, wood stoves, and all home heating systems inspected and cleaned annually by a certified specialist.
- Insulate chimneys and place spark arresters on top. The chimney should be at least three feet above the roof.
- Remove branches hanging above and around the chimney.

FOLLOW LOCAL BURNING LAWS

Before burning debris in a wooded area, make sure you notify local authorities, obtain a burning permit, and follow these guidelines:

- Use an approved incinerator with a safety lid or covering with holes no larger than three-quarters of an inch.
- Create at least a ten-foot clearing around the incinerator before burning debris.
- Have a fire extinguisher or garden hose on hand when burning debris.

During a Wildfire

If a wildfire threatens your home and time permits, take the following precautions.

- Shut off gas at the meter. Only a qualified professional can safely turn the gas back on.
- Seal attic and ground vents with precut plywood or commercial seals.

- Turn off propane tanks.
- Place combustible patio furniture inside.
- Connect a garden hose to an outside tap. Place lawn sprinklers on the roof and near aboveground fuel tanks. Wet the roof.
- Wet or remove shrubs within fifteen feet of your residence.
- Gather fire tools such as a rake, axe, handsaw or chainsaw, bucket, and shovel.
- Back your car into the garage or park it in an open space facing the direction of escape. Shut doors and windows. Leave the key in the ignition and the car doors unlocked. Close garage windows and doors, but leave them unlocked. Disconnect automatic garage door openers.
- Open fireplace damper. Close fireplace screens.
- Close windows, vents, doors, blinds or noncombustible window coverings, and heavy drapes. Remove flammable drapes and curtains.
- Move flammable furniture into the center of the residence away from windows and sliding-glass doors.
- Close all interior doors and windows to prevent drafts.
- Place valuables that will not be damaged by water in a pool or pond. If advised to evacuate, do so immediately. Choose a route away from the fire hazard. Watch for changes in the speed and direction of the fire and smoke.

After a Wildfire

Follow the instructions for recovering from a disaster in Part 5.

For More Information

If you require more information about any of these topics, the following resource may be helpful.

FEMA Publication

Wildfire: Are You Prepared? L-203. Wildfire safety tips, preparedness, and mitigation techniques.

PART 3: TECHNOLOGICAL HAZARDS

Technological hazards include hazardous materials incidents and nuclear power plant failures. Usually, little or no warning precedes incidents involving technological hazards. In many cases, victims may not know they have been affected until many years later. For example, health problems caused by hidden toxic waste sites—like that at Love Canal, near Niagara Falls, New York—surfaced years after initial exposure.

The number of technological incidents is escalating, mainly as a result of the increased number of new substances and the opportunities for human error inherent in the use of these materials.

Use Part 3 to learn what actions to include in your family disaster plan to prepare for and respond to events involving technological hazards. Learn how to use, store, and dispose of household chemicals in a manner that will reduce the potential for injury to people and the environment.

When you complete Part 3, you will be able to:

- Recognize important terms.
- Take protective measures for technological disasters.
- Know what actions to take if an event occurs.
- Identify resources for more information about technological hazards.

3.1. HAZARDOUS MATERIALS INCIDENTS

Chemicals are found everywhere. They purify drinking water, increase crop production, and simplify household chores. But chemicals also can be hazardous to humans or the environment if used or released improperly. Hazards can occur during production, storage, transportation, use, or disposal. You and your community are at risk if a chemical is used unsafely or released in harmful amounts into the environment where you live, work, or play.

Chemical manufacturers are one source of hazardous materials, but there are many others, including service stations, hospitals, and hazardous materials waste sites.

Take Protective Measures

Before a Hazardous Materials Incident

Many communities have Local Emergency Planning Committees (LEPCs) whose responsibilities include collecting information about hazardous materials in the community and making this information available to the public upon request. The LEPCs also are tasked with developing an emergency plan to prepare for and respond to chemical emergencies in the community. Ways the public will be notified and actions the public must take in the event of a release are part of the plan. Contact the LEPCs to find out more about chemical hazards and what needs to be done to minimize the risk to individuals and the community from these materials. The local emergency management office can provide contact information on the LEPCs.

You should add the following supplies to your disaster supplies kit:

- Plastic sheeting.
- Duct tape.
- Scissors.

Review

See section 1.3, Assemble a Disaster Supplies Kit.

During a Hazardous Materials Incident

Listen to local radio or television stations for detailed information and instructions. Follow the instructions carefully. You should stay away from the area to minimize the risk of contamination. Remember that some toxic chemicals are odorless.

If you are

asked to evacuate: Do so immediately.

caught outside: Stay upstream, uphill, and upwind! In general, try to go at least one-half mile (usually eight to ten city blocks) from the danger area. Do not walk into or touch any spilled liquids, airborne mists, or condensed solid chemical deposits.

in a motor vehicle: Stop and seek shelter in a permanent building. If you must remain in your car, keep car windows and vents closed and shut off the air conditioner and heater.

requested to stay indoors:

Close and lock all exterior doors and windows. Close vents, fireplace dampers, and as many interior doors as possible.

Turn off air conditioners and ventilation systems. In large buildings, set ventilation systems to 100 percent recirculation so that no outside air is drawn into the building. If this is not possible, ventilation systems should be turned off.

Go into the preselected shelter room. This room should be aboveground and have the fewest openings to the outside.

Seal the room by covering each window, door, and vent using plastic sheeting and duct tape.

Use material to fill cracks and holes in the room, such as those around pipes.

SHELTER SAFETY FOR SEALED ROOMS

Ten square feet of floor space per person will provide sufficient air to prevent carbon dioxide buildup for up to five hours, assuming a normal breathing rate while resting.

However, local officials are unlikely to recommend the public shelter in a sealed room for more than two to three hours because the effectiveness of such sheltering diminishes with time as the contaminated outside air gradually seeps into the shelter. At this point, evacuation from the area is the better protective action to take.

Also, you should ventilate the shelter when the emergency has passed to avoid breathing contaminated air still inside the shelter.

After a Hazardous Materials Incident

The following are guidelines for the period following a hazardous materials incident.

- Return home only when authorities say it is safe. Open windows and vents and turn on fans to provide ventilation.

- Act quickly if you have come into contact with or have been exposed to hazardous chemicals. Do the following:

  - Follow decontamination instructions from local authorities. You may be advised to take a thorough shower, or you may be advised to stay away from water and follow another procedure.

  - Seek medical treatment for unusual symptoms as soon as possible.

- Place exposed clothing and shoes in tightly sealed containers. Do not allow them to contact other materials. Call local authorities to find out about proper disposal.

- Advise everyone who comes into contact with you that you may have been exposed to a toxic substance.

- Find out from local authorities how to clean up your land and property.
- Report any lingering vapors or other hazards to your local emergency services office.
- Follow the instructions for recovering from a disaster in Part 5.

3.2. HOUSEHOLD CHEMICAL EMERGENCIES

Nearly every household uses products containing hazardous materials or chemicals.

Cleaning Products

- Oven cleaners
- Drain cleaners
- Wood and metal cleaners and polishes
- Toilet cleaners
- Tub, tile, shower cleaners
- Bleach (laundry)
- Pool chemicals

Indoor Pesticides

- Ant sprays and baits
- Cockroach sprays and baits
- Flea repellents and shampoos
- Bug sprays

- Houseplant insecticides
- Moth repellents
- Mouse and rat poisons and baits

Automotive Products

- Motor oil
- Fuel additives
- Carburetor and fuel injection cleaners
- Air-conditioning refrigerants
- Starter fluids
- Automotive batteries
- Transmission and brake fluid
- Antifreeze

Workshop/Painting Supplies

- Adhesives and glues
- Furniture strippers
- Oil- or enamel-based paint
- Stains and finishes
- Paint thinners and turpentine
- Paint strippers and removers
- Photographic chemicals
- Fixatives and other solvents

Lawn and Garden Products

- Herbicides
- Insecticides
- Fungicides/wood preservatives

Miscellaneous

- Batteries
- Mercury thermostats or thermometers
- Fluorescent light bulbs
- Driveway sealer

Other Flammable Products

- Propane tanks and other compressed gas cylinders
- Kerosene
- Home heating oil
- Diesel fuel
- Gas/oil mix
- Lighter fluid

Although the risk of a chemical accident is slight, knowing how to handle these products and how to react during an emergency can reduce the risk of injury.

Take Protective Measures

Before a Household Chemical Emergency

The following are guidelines for buying and storing hazardous household chemicals safely:

- Buy only as much of a chemical as you think you will use. Leftover material can be shared with neighbors or donated to a business, charity, or government agency. For example, excess pesticide could be offered to a greenhouse or garden center, and theater groups often need surplus paint. Some communities have organized waste exchanges where household hazardous chemicals and waste can be swapped or given away.
- Keep products containing hazardous materials in their

original containers and never remove the labels unless the container is corroding. Corroding containers should be re-packaged and clearly labeled.

- Never store hazardous products in food containers.
- Never mix household hazardous chemicals or waste with other products. Incompatibles, such as chlorine bleach and ammonia, may react, ignite, or explode.

Take the following precautions to prevent and respond to accidents:

- Follow the manufacturer's instructions for the proper use of the household chemical.
- Never smoke while using household chemicals.
- Never use hair spray, cleaning solutions, paint products, or pesticides near an open flame (e.g., pilot light, lighted candle, fireplace, wood-burning stove, etc.). Although you may not be able to see or smell them, vapor particles in the air could catch fire or explode.
- Clean up any chemical spill immediately. Use rags to clean up the spill. Wear gloves and eye protection. Allow the fumes in the rags to evaporate outdoors, then dispose of the rags by wrapping them in a newspaper and placing them in a sealed plastic bag in your trash can.
- Dispose of hazardous materials correctly. Take household hazardous waste to a local collection program. Check with your county or state environmental or solid waste agency to learn if there is a household hazardous waste collection program in your area.

Learn to recognize the symptoms of toxic poisoning, which are as follows:

- Difficulty breathing.
- Irritation of the eyes, skin, throat, or respiratory tract.

- Changes in skin color.
- Headache or blurred vision.
- Dizziness.
- Clumsiness or lack of coordination.
- Cramps or diarrhea.

Be prepared to seek medical assistance.

- Post the number of the emergency medical services and the poison control center by all telephones. In an emergency situation, you may not have time to look up critical phone numbers. The national poison control number is (800) 222-1222.

During a Household Chemical Emergency

If there is a danger of fire or explosion:

- Get out of the residence immediately. Do not waste time collecting items or calling the fire department when you are in danger. Call the fire department from outside (a cellular phone or a neighbor's phone) once you are safely away from danger.
- Stay upwind and away from the residence to avoid breathing toxic fumes. If someone has been exposed to a household chemical:
  - Find any containers of the substance that are readily available in order to provide requested information. Call emergency medical services.
  - Follow the emergency operator or dispatcher's first-aid instructions carefully. The first-aid advice found on containers may be out of date or inappropriate. Do not give anything by mouth unless advised to do so by a medical professional.

• Discard clothing that may have been contaminated. Some chemicals may not wash out completely.

CHECKING YOUR HOME

There are probably many hazardous materials throughout your home. Take a tour of your home to see where these materials are located. Use the list of common hazardous household items presented earlier to guide you in your hunt. Once you have located a product, check the label and take the necessary steps to ensure that you are using, storing, and disposing of the material according to the manufacturer's directions. It is critical to store household chemicals in places where children cannot access them. Remember that products such as aerosol cans of hair spray and deodorant, nail polish and nail polish remover, toilet bowl cleaners, and furniture polishes all fall into the category of hazardous materials.

For More Information

If you require more information about any of these topics, the following are resources that may be helpful.

FEMA Publications

Household Hazardous Materials: A Guide for Citizens. IS 55. An independent study resource for parents and teachers. Web-based safety program focused on reducing the number of deaths and injuries in the home. Available online at http://training.fema.gov/emiweb/is/is55.asp.

Chemical Emergencies. A pamphlet promoting awareness of chemical hazards in the home, how to prevent them, and what to do if exposed. Available online at www.fema .gov.

Backgrounder: Hazardous Materials. 0.511. Information sheet available online at www.fema.gov/hazards/hazard ousmaterials/hazmat.shtm.

USFA: Factsheet: Baby-sitters Make the Right Call to EMS. 0510. Available online at www.usfa.fema.gov.

American Red Cross Publications

Chemical Emergencies. Extensive document describing the hazards of household chemicals and what to do in an emergency. Available online at www.redcross.org.

3.3. NUCLEAR POWER PLANTS

Nuclear power plants use the heat generated from nuclear fission in a contained environment to convert water to steam, which powers generators to produce electricity. Nuclear power plants operate in most states in the country and produce about 20 percent of the nation's power. Nearly three million Americans live within ten miles of an operating nuclear power plant.

Although the construction and operation of these facilities are closely monitored and regulated by the Nuclear Regulatory Commission (NRC), accidents are possible. An accident could result in dangerous levels of radiation that could affect the health and safety of the public living near the nuclear power plant.

Local and state governments, federal agencies, and the electric utilities have emergency response plans in the event of a nuclear power plant incident. The plans define two "emergency planning zones." One zone covers an area within a ten-mile radius of the plant, where it is possible that people could be harmed by direct radiation exposure. The second zone covers a broader area, usually up to a fifty-mile radius from the plant, where radioactive materials could contaminate water supplies, food crops, and livestock.

The potential danger from an accident at a nuclear power plant is exposure to radiation. This exposure could come from the release of radioactive material from the plant into the environment, usually characterized by a plume (cloudlike formation) of radioactive gases and particles. The major hazards to people in the vicinity of the plume are radiation exposure to the body from the cloud and particles deposited on the ground, inhalation of radioactive materials, and ingestion of radioactive materials.

Radioactive materials are composed of atoms that are unstable. An unstable atom gives off its excess energy until it becomes stable. The energy emitted is radiation. Each of us is exposed to radiation daily from natural sources, including the sun and the earth. Small traces of radiation are present in food and water. Radiation also is released from man-made sources such as X-ray machines, television sets, and microwave ovens. Radiation has a cumulative effect. The longer a person is exposed to radiation, the greater the effect. A high exposure to radiation can cause serious illness or death.

Minimizing Exposure to Radiation

- Distance—The more distance between you and the source of the radiation, the better. This could be evacuation or remaining indoors to minimize exposure.
- Shielding—The more heavy, dense material between you and the source of the radiation, the better.
- Time—Most radioactivity loses its strength fairly quickly.

If an accident at a nuclear power plant were to release radiation in your area, local authorities would activate warning sirens or another approved alert method. They also would instruct you through the Emergency Alert System (EAS) on local television and radio stations on how to protect yourself.

Know the Terms

Familiarize yourself with these terms to help identify a nuclear power plant emergency.

NOTIFICATION OF UNUSUAL EVENT: A small problem has occurred at the plant. No radiation leak is expected. No action on your part will be necessary.

ALERT: A small problem has occurred, and small amounts of radiation could leak inside the plant. This will not affect you and no action is required.

SITE AREA EMERGENCY: Area sirens may be sounded. Listen to your radio or television for safety information.

GENERAL EMERGENCY: Radiation could leak outside the plant and off the plant site. The sirens will sound. Tune to your local radio or television station for reports. Be prepared to follow instructions promptly.

Take Protective Measures

Before a Nuclear Power Plant Emergency

Obtain public emergency information materials from the power company that operates your local nuclear power plant or your local emergency services office. If you live within ten miles of the power plant, you should receive these materials yearly from the power company or your state or local government.

During a Nuclear Power Plant Emergency

The following are guidelines for what you should do if a nuclear power plant emergency occurs. Keep a battery-powered radio with you at all times and listen to the radio for specific instructions. Close and lock doors and windows.

If you are told to evacuate:

- Keep car windows and vents closed; use recirculating air.

If you are advised to remain indoors:

- Turn off the air conditioner, ventilation fans, furnace, and other air intakes.
- Go to a basement or other underground area, if possible.
- Do not use the telephone unless absolutely necessary.

If you expect you have been exposed to nuclear radiation:

- Change clothes and shoes.
- Put exposed clothing in a plastic bag.
- Seal the bag and place it out of the way.
- Take a thorough shower.
- Keep food in covered containers or in the refrigerator. Food not previously covered should be washed before being put into containers.

After a Nuclear Power Plant Emergency

Seek medical treatment for any unusual symptoms, such as nausea, that may be related to radiation exposure.

Follow the instructions for recovering from a disaster in Part 5.

TECHNOLOGICAL HAZARDS KNOWLEDGE CHECK

Answer the following questions. Check your responses with the answer key below.

1. What are some things you can do to reduce the threat from hazardous materials in your home?
2. What should you do if you are caught at the scene of a hazardous materials incident?
3. What is the telephone number for the National Poison Control Center?
4. What are three ways to minimize radiation exposure?
5. Are there special warning requirements for nuclear power plants? If so, what are they?
6. What does it mean when a nuclear power plant has issued a general emergency? What actions should you take?
7. If you are at home and instructed to shelter-in-place because of a chemical release, where will you go?
8. If you are in a car and unable to seek shelter in a building and a chemical release occurs, what should you do?
9. Who can you contact to find out about hazardous materials stored in your community?
10. What are some common places hazardous materials that may be present in the community?

Answer key:

1.

   a. Learn to identify hazardous materials.
   b. Follow manufacturer's instructions for storage, use, and disposal.
   c. Never store hazardous products in food containers.
   d. Keep products in original containers unless the container is corroding.
   e. Never mix household hazardous chemicals or waste with other products.
   f. Take household hazardous waste to a local collection program.
   g. Never smoke while using household chemicals.

h. Clean up spills immediately with rags.

i. Buy only as much of a chemical as you think you will use.

2.

a. Do not walk into or touch any spilled liquids, airborne mists, or condensed solid chemical deposits.

b. Stay upstream, uphill, and upwind! In general, try to go at least one-half mile (usually eight to ten city blocks) from the danger area.

3. (800) 222-1222

4. Distance, shielding, and time.

5. Yes. Nuclear power plants are required to install sirens or other approved warning systems.

6. Radiation could leak outside the plant and off the plant site. The sirens will sound. Tune to local radio or television station for reports. Be prepared to follow instructions promptly.

7. An aboveground room with the fewest exterior doors and windows.

8. Keep car windows and vents closed and shut off the air conditioner or heater.

9. Local Emergency Planning Committee (LEPC). The local emergency management office can provide contact information for the LEPCs.

10. Agricultural operations and farms, auto service stations and junkyards, chemical manufacturing and storage facilities, construction sites, dry cleaners, electronics manufactures, paint shops, hospitals, hazardous materials waste sites, and transportation routes.

PART 4: TERRORISM

Throughout human history, there have been many threats to the security of nations. These threats have brought about large-scale losses of life, the destruction of property, widespread illness and injury, the displacement of large numbers of people, and devastating economic loss.

Recent technological advances and ongoing international political unrest are components of the increased risk to national security.

Use Part 4 to learn what actions to include in your family disaster plan to prepare for and respond to terrorist threats.

When you complete Part 4, you will be able to:

- Recognize important terms.
- Take protective measures for terrorist threats.
- Know what actions to take if an event occurs.
- Identify resources for more information about terrorist threats.

4.1. GENERAL INFORMATION ABOUT TERRORISM

Terrorism is the use of force or violence against persons or property in violation of the criminal laws of the United States for purposes of intimidation, coercion, or ransom. Terrorists often use threats to:

- create fear among the public;
- try to convince citizens that their government is powerless to prevent terrorism;
- get immediate publicity for their causes.

Acts of terrorism include threats of terrorism; assassinations; kidnappings; hijackings; bomb scares and bombings; cyber attacks (computer-based); and the use of chemical, biological, nuclear, and radiological weapons.

High-risk targets for acts of terrorism include military and civilian government facilities, international airports, large cities, and high-profile landmarks. Terrorists might also target large public gatherings, water and food supplies, utilities, and corporate centers. Further, terrorists are capable of spreading fear by sending explosives or chemical and biological agents through the mail.

Within the immediate area of a terrorist event, you would need to rely on police, fire, and other officials for instructions. However, you can prepare in much the same way you would prepare for other crisis events. The following are general guidelines.

- Be aware of your surroundings.
- Move or leave if you feel uncomfortable or if something does not seem right.
- Take precautions when traveling. Be aware of conspicuous or unusual behavior. Do not accept packages from strangers. Do not leave luggage unattended. You should promptly report unusual behavior, suspicious or unattended packages, and strange devices to the police or security personnel.
- Learn where emergency exits are located in buildings you frequent. Plan how to get out in the event of an emergency.
- Be prepared to do without services you normally depend on—electricity, telephone, natural gas, gasoline pumps, cash registers, ATMs, and Internet transactions.
- Work with building owners to ensure the following items are located on each floor of the building:

  Portable, battery-operated radio and extra batteries.

  Several flashlights and extra batteries.

  First-aid kit and manual.

  Hard hats and dust masks.

  Fluorescent tape to rope off dangerous areas.

4.2. EXPLOSIONS

Terrorists have frequently used explosive devices as one of their most common weapons. Terrorists do not have to look far to find out how to make explosive devices; the information is readily available in books and other information sources. The materials needed for an explosive device can be found in many places including variety, hardware, and auto supply stores. Explosive devices are highly portable using vehicles and humans as a means of transport. They are easily detonated from remote locations or by suicide bombers.

Conventional bombs have been used to damage and destroy financial, political, social, and religious institutions. Attacks have occurred in public places and on city streets, with thousands of people around the world injured and killed.

Parcels that should make you suspicious:

- Are unexpected or from someone unfamiliar to you.
- Have no return address, or have one that can't be verified as legitimate.
- Are marked with restrictive endorsements such as "Personal," "Confidential," or "Do not X-ray."
- Have protruding wires or aluminum foil, strange odors, or stains.
- Show a city or state in the postmark that doesn't match the return address.
- Are of unusual weight given their size, or are lopsided or oddly shaped.
- Are marked with threatening language.
- Have inappropriate or unusual labeling.
- Have excessive postage or packaging material, such as masking tape and string.
- Have misspellings of common words.
- Are addressed to someone no longer with your organization or are otherwise outdated.
- Have incorrect titles or titles without a name.
- Are not addressed to a specific person.
- Have handwritten or poorly typed addresses.

Take Protective Measures

If you receive a telephoned bomb threat, you should do the following.

- Get as much information from the caller as possible.
- Keep the caller on the line and record everything that is said.
- Notify the police and the building management.

During an Explosion

If there is an explosion, you should:

- Get under a sturdy table or desk if things are falling around you. When they stop falling, leave quickly, watching for obviously weakened floors and stairways. As you exit from the building, be especially watchful of falling debris.
- Leave the building as quickly as possible. Do not stop to retrieve personal possessions or make phone calls.
- Do not use elevators.

Once you are out:

- Do not stand in front of windows, glass doors, or other potentially hazardous areas.
- Move away from sidewalks or streets to be used by emergency officials or others still exiting the building.

If you are trapped in debris:

- If possible, use a flashlight to signal your location to rescuers.
- Avoid unnecessary movement so you don't kick up dust.
- Cover your nose and mouth with anything you have on hand.

(Dense-weave cotton material can act as a good filter. Try to breathe through the material.)

- Tap on a pipe or wall so rescuers can hear where you are.
- If possible, use a whistle to signal rescuers.
- Shout only as a last resort. Shouting can cause a person to inhale dangerous amounts of dust.

Review

See safety guidelines for escaping fires in section 2.11.

After an Explosion

Follow the instructions for recovering from a disaster in Part 5.

For More Information

If you require more information about any of these topics, the following resource may be helpful.

American Red Cross Publication

Terrorism, Preparing for the Unexpected. Document providing preparation guidelines for a terrorist attack or similar emergency. Available online at www.redcross.org.

4.3. BIOLOGICAL THREATS

Biological agents are organisms or toxins that can kill or incapacitate people, livestock, and crops. The three basic groups of biological agents that would likely be used as weapons are bacteria, viruses, and toxins. Most biological agents are difficult to grow and maintain. Many break down quickly when exposed to sunlight and other environmental factors, while others, such as anthrax spores, are very long-lived. Biological agents can be dispersed by spraying them into the air, by infecting animals that carry the disease to humans, and by contaminating food and water. Delivery methods include:

- Aerosols—Biological agents are dispersed into the air, forming a fine mist that may drift for miles. Inhaling the agent may cause disease in people or animals.
- Animals—Some diseases are spread by insects and animals, such as fleas, mice, flies, mosquitoes, and livestock.
- Food and water contamination—Some pathogenic organisms and toxins may persist in food and water supplies. Most microbes can be killed, and toxins deactivated, by cooking food and boiling water. Most microbes are killed by boiling water for one minute, but some require longer. Follow official instructions.
- Person-to-person—Spread of a few infectious agents is also possible. Humans have been the source of infection for smallpox, plague, and the Lassa viruses.

Specific information on biological agents is available at the Centers for Disease Control and Prevention's Web site, www.bt .cdc.gov.

Take Protective Measures

Before a Biological Attack

The following are guidelines for what you should do to prepare for a biological threat.

- Check with your doctor to ensure all required or suggested immunizations are up to date. Children and older adults are particularly vulnerable to biological agents.
- Consider installing a High Efficiency Particulate Air (HEPA)

filter in your furnace return duct. These filters remove particles in the 0.3- to 10-micron range and will filter out most biological agents that may enter your house. If you do not have a central heating or cooling system, a stand-alone portable HEPA filter can be used.

FILTRATION IN BUILDINGS

Building owners and managers should determine the type and level of filtration in their structures and the level of protection it provides against biological agents. The National Institute of Occupational Safety and Health (NIOSH) provides technical guidance on this topic in their publication *Guidance for Filtration and Air-Cleaning Systems to Protect Building Environments from Airborne Chemical, Biological, or Radiological Attacks*. To obtain a copy, call (800) 35NIOSH or visit www. cdc.gov/NIOSH/ and request or download NIOSH Publication 2003-136.

Review

See shelter information in section 1.4, Shelter.

During a Biological Attack

In the event of a biological attack, public health officials may not immediately be able to provide information on what you should do. It will take time to determine what the illness is, how it should be treated, and who is in danger. Watch television, listen to radio, or check the Internet for official news and information including signs and symptoms of the disease, areas in danger, if medications or vaccinations are being distributed, and where you should seek medical attention if you become ill.

The first evidence of an attack may be when you notice symptoms of the disease caused by exposure to an agent. Be suspicious of any symptoms you notice, but do not assume that any illness is a result of the attack. Use common sense and practice good hygiene.

If you become aware of an unusual and suspicious substance nearby:

- Move away quickly.
- Wash with soap and water.
- Contact authorities.
- Listen to the media for official instructions.
- Seek medical attention if you become sick.

If you are exposed to a biological agent:

- Remove and bag your clothes and personal items. Follow official instructions for disposal of contaminated items.
- Wash yourself with soap and water and put on clean clothes.
- Seek medical assistance. You may be advised to stay away from others or even be quarantined.

USING HEPA FILTERS

HEPA filters are useful in biological attacks. If you have a central heating and cooling system in your home with a HEPA filter, leave it on if it is running or turn the fan on if it is not running. Moving the air in the house through the filter will help remove the agents from the air. If you have a portable HEPA filter, take it with you to the internal room where you are seeking shelter and turn it on.

If you are in an apartment or office building that has a modern, central heating and cooling system, the system's filtration should provide a relatively safe level of protection from outside biological contaminants. HEPA filters will not filter chemical agents.

After a Biological Attack

In some situations, such as the case of the anthrax letters sent in 2001, people may be alerted to potential exposure. If this is the case, pay close attention to all official warnings and instructions on how to proceed. The delivery of medical services for a biological event may be handled differently to respond to increased demand. The basic public health procedures and medical protocols for handling exposure to biological agents are the same as for any infectious disease. It is important for you to pay attention to official instructions via radio, television, and emergency alert systems.

Review

See section 1.1, Getting Informed.

4.4. CHEMICAL THREATS

Chemical agents are poisonous vapors, aerosols, liquids, and solids that have toxic effects on people, animals, or plants. They can be released by bombs or sprayed from aircraft, boats, and vehicles. They can be used as a liquid to create a hazard to people and the environment. Some chemical agents may be odorless and tasteless. They can have an immediate effect (a few seconds to a few minutes) or a delayed effect (two to forty-eight hours). While potentially lethal, chemical agents are difficult to deliver in lethal concentrations. Outdoors, the agents often dissipate rapidly. Chemical agents also are difficult to produce.

A chemical attack could come without warning. Signs of a chemical release include people having difficulty breathing; experiencing eye irritation; losing coordination; becoming nauseated; or having a burning sensation in the nose, throat, and lungs. Also, the presence of many dead insects or birds may indicate a chemical agent release.

Take Protective Measures

Before a Chemical Attack

The following are guidelines for what you should do to prepare for a chemical threat:

- Check your disaster supplies kit to make sure it includes:

  A roll of duct tape and scissors.

  Plastic for doors, windows, and vents for the room in which you will shelter-in-place. To save critical time during an emergency, premeasure and cut the plastic sheeting for each opening.
- Choose an internal room to shelter, preferably one without windows and on the highest level.

During a Chemical Attack

The following are guidelines for what you should do in a chemical attack.

If you are instructed to remain in your home or office building, you should do the following:

- Close doors and windows and turn off all ventilation, including furnaces, air conditioners, vents, and fans.
- Seek shelter in an internal room and take your disaster supplies kit.
- Seal the room with duct tape and plastic sheeting.
- Listen to your radio for instructions from authorities.

Review

See "Shelter Safety for Sealed Rooms" in section 3.1, Hazardous Materials Incidents.

If you are caught in or near a contaminated area, you should:

- Move away immediately in a direction upwind of the source.
- Find shelter as quickly as possible.

After a Chemical Attack

Decontamination is needed within minutes of exposure to minimize health consequences. Do not leave the safety of a shelter to go outdoors to help others until authorities announce it is safe to do so.

A person affected by a chemical agent requires immediate medical attention from a professional. If medical help is not immediately available, decontaminate yourself and assist in decontaminating others.

Decontamination guidelines are as follows:

- Use extreme caution when helping others who have been exposed to chemical agents.
- Remove all clothing and other items in contact with the body. Contaminated clothing normally removed over the head should be cut off to avoid contact with the eyes, nose, and mouth. Put contaminated clothing and items into a plastic bag and seal it. Decontaminate hands using soap and water. Remove eyeglasses or contact lenses. Put glasses in a pan of household bleach to decontaminate them, and then rinse and dry.
- Flush eyes with water.
- Gently wash face and hair with soap and water before thoroughly rinsing with water.
- Decontaminate other body areas likely to have been contaminated. Blot (do not swab or scrape) with a cloth soaked in soapy water and rinse with clear water.
- Change into uncontaminated clothes. Clothing stored in drawers or closets is likely to be uncontaminated.

- Proceed to a medical facility for screening and professional treatment.

4.5. NUCLEAR BLASTS

A nuclear blast is an explosion with intense light and heat, a damaging pressure wave, and widespread radioactive material that can contaminate the air, water, and ground surfaces for miles around. A nuclear device can range from a weapon carried by an intercontinental missile launched by a hostile nation or terrorist organization, to a small portable nuclear device transported by an individual. All nuclear devices cause deadly effects when exploded, including blinding light, intense heat (thermal radiation), initial nuclear radiation, blast, fires started by the heat pulse, and secondary fires caused by the destruction.

Hazards of Nuclear Devices

The extent, nature, and arrival time of these hazards are difficult to predict. The geographical dispersion of hazard effects will be defined by the following:

- Size of the device. A more powerful bomb will produce more distant effects.
- Height above the ground the device was detonated. This will determine the extent of blast effects.
- Nature of the surface beneath the explosion. Some materials are more likely to become radioactive and airborne than others. Flat areas are more susceptible to blast effects.
- Existing meteorological conditions. Wind speed and direction will affect arrival time of fallout; precipitation may wash fallout from the atmosphere.

Radioactive Fallout

Even if individuals are not close enough to the nuclear blast to be affected by the direct impacts, they may be affected by radioactive fallout. Any nuclear blast results in some fallout. Blasts that occur near the earth's surface create much greater amounts of fallout than blasts that occur at higher altitudes. This is because the tremendous heat produced from a nuclear blast causes an up-draft of air that forms the familiar mushroom cloud. When a blast occurs near the earth's surface, millions of vaporized dirt particles also are drawn into the cloud. As the heat diminishes, radioactive materials that have vaporized condense on the particles and fall back to earth. The phenomenon is called radioactive fallout. This fallout material decays over a long period of time, and is the main source of residual nuclear radiation.

Fallout from a nuclear explosion may be carried by wind currents for hundreds of miles if the right conditions exist. Effects from even a small portable device exploded at ground level can be potentially deadly.

Nuclear radiation cannot be seen, smelled, or otherwise detected by normal senses. Radiation can only be detected by radiation monitoring devices. This makes radiological emergencies different from other types of emergencies, such as floods or hurricanes. Monitoring can project the fallout arrival times, which will be announced through official warning channels. However, any increase in surface buildup of gritty dust and dirt should be a warning for taking protective measures.

Electromagnetic Pulse

In addition to other effects, a nuclear weapon detonated in or above the earth's atmosphere can create an electromagnetic pulse (EMP), a high-density electrical field. An EMP acts like a stroke of lightning but is stronger, faster, and shorter. An EMP can seriously damage electronic devices connected to power sources or antennae. This includes communication systems, computers, electrical appliances, and automobile or aircraft ignition systems. The damage could range from a minor interruption to actual burnout of components. Most electronic equipment within one thousand miles of a high-altitude nuclear detonation could be affected. Battery-powered radios with short antennae generally would not be affected. Although an EMP is unlikely to harm most people, it could harm those with pacemakers or other implanted electronic devices.

Protection from a Nuclear Blast

The danger of a massive strategic nuclear attack on the United States is predicted by experts to be less likely today. However, terrorism, by nature, is unpredictable.

If there were a threat of an attack, people living near potential targets could be advised to evacuate or they could decide on their own to evacuate to an area not considered a likely target. Protection from radioactive fallout would require taking shelter in an underground area or in the middle of a large building.

In general, potential targets include:

- Strategic missile sites and military bases.
- Centers of government such as Washington, D.C., and state capitals.
- Important transportation and communication centers.
- Manufacturing, industrial, technology, and financial centers.
- Petroleum refineries, electrical power plants, and chemical plants.
- Major ports and airfields.

The three factors for protecting oneself from radiation and fallout are distance, shielding, and time.

- Distance—The more distance between you and the fallout particles, the better. An underground area such as a home or office building basement offers more protection than the first floor of a building. A floor near the middle of a high-rise may be better, depending on what is nearby at that level on which significant fallout particles would collect. Flat roofs collect fallout particles so the top floor is not a good choice, nor is a floor adjacent to a neighboring flat roof.

- Shielding—The heavier and denser the materials (thick walls, concrete, bricks, books, and earth) between you and the fallout particles, the better.
- Time—Fallout radiation loses its intensity fairly rapidly. In time, you will be able to leave the fallout shelter. Radioactive fallout poses the greatest threat to people during the first two weeks, by which time it has declined to about 1 percent of its initial radiation level.

Remember that any protection, however temporary, is better than none at all, and the more shielding, distance, and time you can take advantage of, the better.

Take Protective Measures

Before a Nuclear Blast

To prepare for a nuclear blast, you should do the following:

- Find out from officials if any public buildings in your community have been designated as fallout shelters. If none have been designated, make your own list of potential shelters near your home, workplace, and school. These places would include basements or the windowless center area of middle floors in high-rise buildings, as well as subways and tunnels.
- If you live in an apartment building or high-rise, talk to the manager about the safest place in the building for sheltering and about providing for building occupants until it is safe to go out.
- During periods of increased threat, increase your disaster supplies to be adequate for up to two weeks.

Taking shelter during a nuclear blast is absolutely necessary. There are two kinds of shelters—blast and fallout. The following describes the two kinds of shelters:

- Blast shelters are specifically constructed to offer some protection against blast pressure, initial radiation, heat, and fire. But even a blast shelter cannot withstand a direct hit from a nuclear explosion.
- Fallout shelters do not need to be specially constructed for protecting against fallout. They can be any protected space, provided that the walls and roof are thick and dense enough to absorb the radiation given off by fallout particles.

Review

See shelter requirements in section 1.4, Shelter.

During a Nuclear Blast

The following are guidelines for what to do in the event of a nuclear explosion.

If an attack warning is issued:

- Take cover as quickly as you can, below ground if possible, and stay there until instructed to do otherwise.
- Listen for official information and follow instructions.

If you are caught outside and unable to get inside immediately:

- Do not look at the flash or fireball—it can blind you.
- Take cover behind anything that might offer protection.
- Lie flat on the ground and cover your head. If the explosion is some distance away, it could take thirty seconds or more for the blast wave to hit.

- Take shelter as soon as you can, even if you are many miles from ground zero where the attack occurred—radioactive fallout can be carried by the winds for hundreds of miles. Remember the three protective factors: distance, shielding, and time.

After a Nuclear Blast

Decay rates of the radioactive fallout are the same for any size nuclear device. However, the amount of fallout will vary based on the size of the device and its proximity to the ground. Therefore, it might be necessary for those in the areas with the highest radiation levels to shelter for up to a month.

The heaviest fallout would be limited to the area at or downwind from the explosion, and 80 percent of the fallout would occur during the first twenty-four hours.

People in most of the areas that would be affected could be allowed to come out of shelter within a few days and, if necessary, evacuate to unaffected areas.

Remember the following:

- Keep listening to the radio and television for news about what to do, where to go, and places to avoid.
- Stay away from damaged areas. Stay away from areas marked "radiation hazard" or "HAZMAT." Remember that radiation cannot be seen, smelled, or otherwise detected by human senses.
- Follow the instructions for returning home in Part 5.

4.6. RADIOLOGICAL DISPERSION DEVICES (RDD)

Terrorist use of a radiological dispersion device (RDD)—often called a "dirty nuke" or "dirty bomb"—is considered far more likely than use of a nuclear explosive device. An RDD combines a conventional explosive device—such as a bomb—with radioactive material. It is designed to scatter dangerous and sublethal amounts of radioactive material over a general area. Such RDDs appeal to terrorists because they require limited technical knowledge to build and deploy compared to a nuclear device. Also, the radioactive materials in RDDs are widely used in medicine, agriculture, industry, and research, and are easier to obtain than weapons-grade uranium or plutonium.

The primary purposes of terrorist use of an RDD are to cause psychological fear and economic disruption. Some devices could cause fatalities from exposure to radioactive materials. Depending on the speed at which the area of the RDD detonation was evacuated or how successful people were at sheltering-in-place, the number of deaths and injuries from an RDD might not be substantially greater than from a conventional bomb explosion.

The size of the affected area and the level of destruction caused by an RDD would depend on the sophistication and size of the conventional bomb, the type of radioactive material used, the quality and quantity of the radioactive material, and the local meteorological conditions—primarily wind and precipitation. The area affected could be placed off-limits to the public for several months during cleanup efforts.

Take Protective Measures

Before an RDD Event

There is no way of knowing how much warning time there would be before an attack by terrorists using an RDD, so being prepared in advance and knowing what to do and when is important. Take the same protective measures you would for fallout resulting from a nuclear blast.

Review

See section 4.5, Nuclear Blasts.

During an RDD Event

While the explosive blast will be immediately obvious, the presence of radiation will not be known until trained personnel with specialized equipment are on the scene. Whether you are indoors or outdoors, home or at work, be extra cautious. It would be safer to assume radiological contamination has occurred—particularly in an urban setting or near other likely terrorist targets—and take the proper precautions. As with any radiation, you want to avoid or limit exposure. This is particularly true of inhaling radioactive dust that results from the explosion. As you seek shelter from any location (indoors or outdoors) and there is visual dust or other contaminants in the air, breathe through the cloth of your shirt or coat to limit your exposure. If you manage to avoid breathing radioactive dust, your proximity to the radioactive particles may still result in some radiation exposure.

If the explosion or radiological release occurs inside the building you are in, get out immediately and seek safe shelter. Otherwise, if you are:

OUTDOORS

- Seek shelter indoors immediately in the nearest undamaged building.
- If appropriate shelter is not available, move as rapidly as is safe upwind and away from the location of the explosive blast. Then, seek appropriate shelter as soon as possible.
- Listen for official instructions and follow directions.

INDOORS

- If you have time, turn off ventilation and heating systems, close windows, vents, fireplace dampers, exhaust fans, and clothes dryer vents. Retrieve your disaster supplies kit and a battery-powered radio and take them to your shelter room.

- Seek shelter immediately, preferably underground or in an interior room of a building, placing as much distance and dense shielding as possible between you and the outdoors where the radioactive material may be.
- Seal windows and external doors that do not fit snugly with duct tape to reduce infiltration of radioactive particles. Plastic sheeting will not provide shielding from radioactivity nor from blast effects of a nearby explosion.
- Listen for official instructions and follow directions.

After an RDD Event

After finding safe shelter, those who may have been exposed to radioactive material should decontaminate themselves. To do this, remove and bag your clothing (and isolate the bag away from you and others), and shower thoroughly with soap and water. Seek medical attention after officials indicate it is safe to leave shelter.

Contamination from an RDD event could affect a wide area, depending on the amount of conventional explosives used, the quantity and type of radioactive material released, and meteorological conditions. Thus, radiation dissipation rates vary, but radiation from an RDD will likely take longer to dissipate due to a potentially larger localized concentration of radioactive material.

Follow these additional guidelines after an RDD event:

- Continue listening to your radio or watch the television for instructions from local officials, whether you have evacuated or sheltered-in-place.
- Do not return to or visit an RDD incident location for any reason.
- Follow the instructions for recovering from a disaster in Part 5.

TERRORISM KNOWLEDGE CHECK

Answer the following questions. Check your responses with the answer key below.

1. What would you do, if you were at work and . . .
   a. there was an explosion in the building?
   b. you received a package in the mail that you considered suspicious?
   c. you received a telephone call that was a bomb threat?
2. If caught outside during a nuclear blast, what should you do?
3. What are the three key factors for protection from nuclear blast and fallout?
4. If you take shelter in your own home, what kind of room would be safest during a chemical or biological attack?
5. In case of a chemical attack, what extra items should you have in your disaster supplies kit?

Answer key:

1.
   a. Shelter from falling debris under a desk and then follow evacuation procedures.
   b. Clear the area and notify the police immediately.
   c. Keep the caller on the line and record everything that was said.
2.
   • Don't look at the flash.
   • Take cover behind anything that offers protection.
   • Lay flat on the ground.
   • Cover your head.
3. Distance, shielding, time.
4. An interior room on the uppermost level, preferably without windows.
5. Plastic sheeting, duct tape, and scissors.

NATIONAL TERRORISM ADVISORY SYSTEM

The "color coded" Homeland Security advisory system has been replaced by the National Terrorism Advisory System, and information about the National Terrorism Advisory System has been provided. More details about the system and how you can help is available at http://www.dhs.gov/files/publications/ntas-public -guide.shtm.

The National Terrorism Advisory System, or NTAS, replaces the color-coded Homeland Security Advisory System (HSAS). This new system will more effectively communicate information about terrorist threats by providing timely, detailed information to the public, government agencies, first responders, airports and other transportation hubs, and the private sector.

It recognizes that Americans all share responsibility for the nation's security, and should always be aware of the heightened risk of terrorist attack in the United States and what they should do.

NTAS ALERTS

IMMINENT THREAT ALERT

Warns of a credible, specific, and impending terrorist threat against the United States.

ELEVATED THREAT ALERT

Warns of a credible terrorist threat against the United States.

After reviewing the available information, the Secretary of Homeland Security will decide, in coordination with other federal entities, whether an NTAS Alert should be issued.

NTAS Alerts will only be issued when credible information is available.

These alerts will include a clear statement that there is an **imminent threat** or **elevated threat**. Using available information, the alerts will provide a concise summary of the potential threat, information about actions being taken to ensure public safety, and recommended steps that individuals, communities, businesses, and governments can take to help prevent, mitigate, or respond to the threat.

The NTAS Alerts will be based on the nature of the threat: in some cases, alerts will be sent directly to law enforcement or affected areas of the private sector, while in others, alerts will be issued more broadly to the American people through both official and media channels.

SUNSET PROVISION

An individual threat alert is issued for a specific time period and then automatically expires. It may be extended if new information becomes available or the threat evolves.

NTAS Alerts contain a **sunset provision** indicating a specific date when the alert expires—there will not be a constant NTAS Alert or blanket warning that there is an overarching threat. If threat information changes for an alert, the Secretary of Homeland Security may announce an updated NTAS Alert. All changes, including the announcement that cancels an NTAS Alert, will be distributed the same way as the original alert.

THE NTAS ALERT—HOW CAN YOU HELP?

TERRORISM INFORMATION

Terrorism information and intelligence is based on the collection, analysis, and reporting of a range of sources and methods. While intelligence may indicate that a threat is credible, specific details may still not be known. As such,

Americans should continue to stay informed and vigilant throughout the duration of an NTAS Alert.

Each alert provides information to the public about the threat, including, if available, the geographic region, mode of transportation, or critical infrastructure potentially affected by the threat; protective actions being taken by authorities, and steps that individuals and communities can take to protect themselves and their families, and help prevent, mitigate, or respond to the threat.

Citizens should report suspicious activity to their local law enforcement authorities. The "If You See Something, Say Something™" campaign across the United States encourages all citizens to be vigilant for indicators of potential terrorist activity, and to follow NTAS Alerts for information about threats in specific places or for individuals exhibiting certain types of suspicious activity. Visit www.dhs. gov/ifyouseesomethingsaysomething to learn more about the campaign.

Citizen Guidance on the Homeland Security Advisory System*
PLEASE NOTE: The following advice from the old "color code" system has been left in place because it provides good information about what you should do when there are risks. The old color code system has been criticized but the colors at least made it easy for a citizen to gauge the risk and take action.

Green—Low Risk

- Develop a family emergency plan. Share it with family and friends, and practice the plan. Visit www.Ready.gov for help creating a plan.

*Developed with input from the American Red Cross.

- Create an emergency supply kit for your household.
- Be informed. Visit www.Ready.gov or obtain a copy of *Preparing Makes Sense, Get Ready Now* by calling (800) BE-READY.
- Know where to shelter and how to turn off utilities (power, gas, and water) to your home.
- Examine volunteer opportunities in your community, such as Citizen Corps, Volunteers in Police Service, Neighborhood Watch, or others, and donate your time. Consider completing an American Red Cross first aid or CPR course, or a Community Emergency Response Team (CERT) course.

Blue—Guarded Risk

- Complete recommended steps at level green.
- Review stored disaster supplies and replace items that are outdated.
- Be alert to suspicious activity and report it to proper authorities.

Yellow—Elevated Risk

- Complete recommended steps at levels green and blue.
- Ensure disaster supplies are stocked and ready.
- Check telephone numbers in family emergency plan and update as necessary.
- Develop alternate routes to/from work or school and practice them.
- Continue to be alert for suspicious activity and report it to authorities.

Orange—High Risk

- Complete recommended steps at lower levels.
- Exercise caution when traveling, pay attention to travel advisories.

- Review your family emergency plan and make sure all family members know what to do.
- Be Patient. Expect some delays, baggage searches, and restrictions at public buildings.
- Check on neighbors or others who might need assistance in an emergency.

Red—Severe Risk

- Complete all recommended actions at lower levels.
- Listen to local emergency management officials.
- Stay tuned to TV or radio for current information/instructions.
- Be prepared to shelter or evacuate, as instructed.
- Expect traffic delays and restrictions.
- Provide volunteer services only as requested.
- Contact your school/business to determine status of work day.

For More Information

If you require more information about any of these topics, the following resource may be helpful.

Publication

American Red Cross: Homeland Security Advisory System Recommendations for Individuals, Families, Neighborhoods, Schools, and Businesses. Explanation of preparedness activities for each population. Available online at www .redcross.org.

KNOWLEDGE CHECK

1. By following the instructions in this guide, you should now have the following:

   • A family disaster plan that sets forth what you and your family need to do to prepare for and respond to all types of hazards.

   • A disaster supplies kit filled with items you would need to sustain you and your family for at least three days, maybe more.

   • Knowledge of your community warning systems and what you should do when these are activated.

   • An understanding of why evacuations are necessary and what you would need to do in the case of an evacuation.

   • Identification of where the safest shelters are for the various hazards.

   Compare the above actions with the personal action guidelines for each of the threat levels. Determine how well you are prepared for each of the five levels.

2. What is the current threat level?

   Hint: To determine the current threat level, check your cable news networks or visit www.dhs.gov. Keep your family informed when changes in the threat level occur, and go over the personal actions you need to take.

PART 5: RECOVERING FROM DISASTER

HEALTH AND SAFETY GUIDELINES

Recovering from a disaster is usually a gradual process. Safety is a primary issue, as are mental and physical well-being. If assistance is available, knowing how to access it makes the process faster and less stressful. This section offers some general advice on steps to take after disaster strikes in order to begin getting your home, your community, and your life back to normal.

Your first concern after a disaster is your family's health and safety. You need to consider possible safety issues and monitor family health and well-being.

Aiding the Injured

- Check for injuries. Do not attempt to move seriously injured persons unless they are in immediate danger of death or further injury. If you must move an unconscious person, first stabilize the neck and back, then call for help immediately.
- If the victim is not breathing, carefully position the victim for artificial respiration, clear the airway, and commence mouth-to-mouth resuscitation.
- Maintain body temperature with blankets. Be sure the victim does not become overheated.
- Never try to feed liquids to an unconscious person.

Health

- Be aware of exhaustion. Don't try to do too much at once. Set priorities and pace yourself. Get enough rest.
- Drink plenty of clean water.
- Eat well.
- Wear sturdy work boots and gloves.
- Wash your hands thoroughly with soap and clean water often when working in debris.

Safety Issues

- Be aware of new safety issues created by the disaster. Watch for washed-out roads, contaminated buildings, contaminated water, gas leaks, broken glass, damaged electrical wiring, and slippery floors.
- Inform local authorities about health and safety issues, including chemical spills, downed power lines, washed-out roads, smoldering insulation, and dead animals.

Returning Home

Returning home can be both physically and mentally challenging. Above all, use caution. Here are some general tips.

- Keep a battery-powered radio with you so you can listen for emergency updates and news reports.
- Use a battery-powered flashlight to inspect a damaged home. *Note:* The flashlight should be turned on outside before entering—the battery may produce a spark that could ignite leaking gas, if present.
- Watch out for animals, especially poisonous snakes. Use a stick to poke through debris.
- Use the phone only to report life-threatening emergencies.
- Stay off the streets. If you must go out, watch for fallen objects; downed electrical wires; and weakened walls, bridges, roads, and sidewalks.

Before You Enter Your Home

Walk carefully around the outside and check for loose power lines, gas leaks, and structural damage. If you have any doubts about safety, have your residence inspected by a qualified building inspector or structural engineer before entering.

Do not enter if:

- you smell gas;
- floodwaters remain around the building;
- your home was damaged by fire and the authorities have not declared it safe. When you go inside your home, there are certain things you should and should not do.

Going Inside Your Home

Enter the home carefully and check for damage. Be aware of loose boards and slippery floors. The following items are other things to check inside your home.

- Natural gas. If you smell gas or hear a hissing or blowing sound, open a window and leave immediately. Turn off the main gas valve from the outside, if you can. Call the gas company from a neighbor's residence. If you shut off the gas supply at the main valve, you will need a professional to turn it back on. Do not smoke or use oil, gas lanterns, candles, or torches for lighting inside a damaged home until you are sure there is no leaking gas or other flammable materials present.

- Sparks, broken or frayed wires. Check the electrical system unless you are wet, standing in water, or unsure of your safety. If possible, turn off the electricity at the main fuse box or circuit breaker. If the situation is unsafe, leave the building and call for help. Do not turn on the lights until you are sure they're safe to use. You may want to have an electrician inspect your wiring.

- Roof, foundation, and chimney cracks. If it looks like the building may collapse, leave immediately.

- Appliances. If appliances are wet, turn off the electricity at the main fuse box or circuit breaker. Then, unplug appliances and let them dry out. Have appliances checked by a professional before using them again. Also, have the electrical system checked by an electrician before turning the power back on.

- Water and sewage systems. If pipes are damaged, turn off the main water valve. Check with local authorities before using any water; the water could be contaminated. Pump out wells and have the water tested by authorities before drinking. Do not flush toilets until you know that sewage lines are intact.

- Food and other supplies. Throw out all food and other supplies that you suspect may have become contaminated or come into contact with floodwater.
- Your basement. If your basement has flooded, pump it out gradually (about one-third of the water per day) to avoid damage. The walls may collapse and the floor may buckle if the basement is pumped out while the surrounding ground is still waterlogged.
- Around the house. Be alert for objects that may fall; open cabinets carefully. Clean up household chemical spills and disinfect items that may have been contaminated by raw sewage, bacteria, or chemicals. Also clean salvageable items.

Be sure to call your insurance agent as soon as possible. Take pictures of damages and keep good records of repair and cleaning costs.

Being Wary of Wildlife and Other Animals

Disasters and life-threatening situations will exacerbate the unpredictable nature of wild animals. To protect yourself and your family, learn how to deal with wildlife.

Guidelines

- Do not approach or attempt to help an injured or stranded animal. Call your local animal control office or wildlife resource office.
- Do not corner wild animals or try to rescue them. Wild animals will likely feel threatened and may endanger themselves by dashing off into floodwaters, fire, and so forth.
- Do not approach wild animals that have taken refuge in your home. Wild animals such as snakes, opossums, and raccoons often seek refuge from floodwaters on upper levels of homes and have been known to remain after water recedes. If you encounter animals in this situation, open a

window or provide another escape route and the animal will likely leave on its own. Do not attempt to capture or handle the animal. Should the animal stay, call your local animal control office or wildlife resource office.

- Do not attempt to move a dead animal. Animal carcasses can present serious health risks. Contact your local emergency management office or health department for help and instructions.
- If bitten by an animal, seek immediate medical attention.

Seeking Disaster Assistance

Throughout the recovery period, it is important to monitor local radio or television reports and other media sources for information about where to get emergency housing, food, first aid, clothing, and financial assistance. The following section provides general information about the kinds of assistance that may be available.

Direct Assistance

Direct assistance to individuals and families may come from any number of organizations, including:

- American Red Cross
- Salvation Army
- Other volunteer organizations

The Federal Role

The above organizations provide food, shelter, and supplies and assist in cleanup efforts. In the most severe disasters, the federal government is also called in to help individuals and families with temporary housing, counseling (for postdisaster trauma), low-interest loans and grants, and other assistance. The federal government also has programs that help small businesses and farmers.

Most federal assistance becomes available when the president of the United States declares a "Major Disaster" for the affected area at the request of a state governor. FEMA will provide information through the media and community outreach about federal assistance and how to apply.

Coping with Disaster

The emotional toll that disaster brings can sometimes be even more devastating than the financial strains of damage and loss of home, business, or personal property.

Understand Disaster Events

- Everyone who sees or experiences a disaster is affected by it in some way.
- It is normal to feel anxious about your own safety and that of your family and close friends.
- Profound sadness, grief, and anger are normal reactions to an abnormal event.
- Acknowledging your feelings helps you recover.
- Focusing on your strengths and abilities helps you heal.
- Accepting help from community programs and resources is healthy.
- Everyone has different needs and different ways of coping.
- It is common to want to strike back at people who have caused great pain.

Children and older adults are of special concern in the aftermath of disasters. Even individuals who experience a disaster "secondhand" through exposure to extensive media coverage can be affected.

Contact local faith-based organizations, voluntary agencies, or professional counselors for counseling. Additionally, FEMA and state and local governments of the affected area may provide crisis counseling assistance.

Recognize Signs of Disaster-Related Stress

When adults have the following signs, they might need crisis counseling or stress management assistance.

- Difficulty communicating thoughts.
- Difficulty sleeping.
- Difficulty maintaining balance in their lives.
- Low threshold of frustration.
- Increased use of drugs/alcohol.
- Limited attention span.
- Poor work performance.
- Headaches/stomach problems.
- Tunnel vision/muffled hearing.
- Colds or flulike symptoms.
- Disorientation or confusion.
- Difficulty concentrating.
- Reluctance to leave home.
- Depression, sadness.
- Feelings of hopelessness.
- Mood swings and easy bouts of crying.
- Overwhelming guilt and self-doubt.
- Fear of crowds, strangers, or being alone.

Ease Disaster-Related Stress

The following are ways to ease disaster-related stress.

- Talk with someone about your feelings—anger, sorrow, and other emotions—even though it may be difficult.
- Seek help from professional counselors who deal with post-disaster stress.
- Do not hold yourself responsible for the disastrous event or be frustrated because you feel you cannot help directly in the rescue work.

- Take steps to promote your own physical and emotional healing by healthy eating, rest, exercise, relaxation, and meditation.
- Maintain a normal family and daily routine, limiting demanding responsibilities on yourself and your family.
- Spend time with family and friends.
- Participate in memorials.
- Use existing support groups of family, friends, and religious institutions.
- Ensure you are ready for future events by restocking your disaster supplies kits and updating your family disaster plan. Doing these positive actions can be comforting.

Helping Children Cope with Disaster

Disasters can leave children feeling frightened, confused, and insecure. Whether a child has personally experienced trauma, has merely seen the event on television, or has heard it discussed by adults, it is important for parents and teachers to be informed and ready to help if reactions to stress begin to occur.

Children may respond to disaster by demonstrating fears, sadness, or behavioral problems. Younger children may return to earlier behavior patterns, such as bed-wetting, sleep problems, and separation anxiety. Older children may also display anger, aggression, school problems, or withdrawal. Some children who have only indirect contact with the disaster but witness it on television may develop distress.

Who Is at Risk?

For many children, reactions to disasters are brief and represent normal reactions to "abnormal events." A smaller number of children can be at risk for more enduring psychological distress as a function of three major risk factors:

- Direct exposure to the disaster, such as being evacuated, observing injuries or death of others, or experiencing injury along with fearing one's life is in danger.
- Loss/grief: This relates to the death or serious injury of family or friends.
- Ongoing stress from the secondary effects of disaster, such as temporarily living elsewhere, loss of friends and social networks, loss of personal property, parental unemployment, and costs incurred during recovery to return the family to predisaster life and living conditions.

What Creates Vulnerabilities in Children?

In most cases, depending on the risk factors above, distressing responses are temporary. In the absence of severe threat to life, injury, loss of loved ones, or secondary problems such as loss of home, moves, etc., symptoms usually diminish over time. For those that were directly exposed to the disaster, reminders of the disaster such as high winds, smoke, cloudy skies, sirens, or other things may cause upsetting feelings to return. Having a prior history of some type of traumatic event or severe stress may contribute to these feelings.

Children's coping with disaster or emergencies is often tied to the way parents cope. They can detect adults' fears and sadness. Parents and adults can make disasters less traumatic for children by taking steps to manage their own feelings and plans for coping. Parents are almost always the best source of support for children in disasters. One way to establish a sense of control and to build confidence in children before a disaster is to engage and involve them in preparing a family disaster plan. After a disaster, children can contribute to a family recovery plan.

Review

See Part 1, Basic Preparedness.

A Child's Reaction to Disaster by Age

Below are common reactions in children after a disaster or traumatic event.

- Birth through two years: When children are preverbal and experience a trauma, they do not have the words to describe the event or their feelings. However, they can retain memories of particular sights, sounds, or smells. Infants may react to trauma by being irritable, crying more than usual, or wanting to be held and cuddled. The biggest influence on children of this age is how their parents cope. As children get older, their play may involve acting out elements of the traumatic event that occurred several years in the past and was seemingly forgotten.

- Preschool—three through six years: Preschool children often feel helpless and powerless in the face of an overwhelming event. Because of their age and small size, they lack the ability to protect themselves or others. As a result, they feel intense fear and insecurity about being separated from caregivers. Preschoolers cannot grasp the concept of permanent loss. They can see consequences as being reversible or permanent. In the weeks following a traumatic event, preschoolers' play activities may reenact the incident or the disaster over and over again.

- School age—seven through ten years: The school-age child has the ability to understand the permanence of loss. Some children become intensely preoccupied with the details of a traumatic event and want to talk about it continually. This preoccupation can interfere with the child's concentration at school and academic performance may decline. At school, children may hear inaccurate information from peers. They may display a wide range of reactions—sadness, generalized fear, or specific fears of the disaster happening again, guilt over action or inaction during the disaster, anger that the event was not prevented, or fantasies of playing rescuer.

- Preadolescence to adolescence—eleven through eighteen years: As children grow older, they develop a more sophisticated understanding of the disaster event. Their responses are more similar to adults. Teenagers may become involved in dangerous, risk-taking behaviors, such as reckless driving, or alcohol or drug use. Others can become fearful of leaving home and avoid previous levels of activities. Much of adolescence is focused on moving out into the world. After a trauma, the world can seem more dangerous and unsafe. A teenager may feel overwhelmed by intense emotions and yet feel unable to discuss them with others.

Meeting the Child's Emotional Needs

Children's reactions are influenced by the behavior, thoughts, and feelings of adults. Adults should encourage children and adolescents to share their thoughts and feelings about the incident. Clarify misunderstandings about risk and danger by listening to children's concerns and answering questions. Maintain a sense of calm by validating children's concerns and perceptions and with discussion of concrete plans for safety.

Listen to what the child is saying. If a young child is asking questions about the event, answer them simply without the elaboration needed for an older child or adult. Some children are comforted by knowing more or less information than others; decide what level of information your particular child needs. If a child has difficulty expressing feelings, allow the child to draw a picture or tell a story of what happened.

Try to understand what is causing anxieties and fears. Be aware that following a disaster, children are most afraid that:

- the event will happen again;
- someone close to them will be killed or injured;
- they will be left alone or separated from the family.

Reassuring Children after a Disaster

Suggestions to help reassure children include the following:

- Personal contact is reassuring. Hug and touch your children.
- Calmly provide factual information about the recent disaster and current plans for insuring their safety along with recovery plans.
- Encourage your children to talk about their feelings.
- Spend extra time with your children such as at bedtime.
- Reestablish your daily routine for work, school, play, meals, and rest.
- Involve your children by giving them specific chores to help them feel they are helping to restore family and community life.
- Praise and recognize responsible behavior.
- Understand that your children will have a range of reactions to disasters.
- Encourage your children to help update your family disaster plan.

If you have tried to create a reassuring environment by following the steps above, but your child continues to exhibit stress, if the reactions worsen over time, or if they cause interference with daily behavior at school, at home, or with other relationships, it may be appropriate to talk to a professional. You can get professional help from the child's primary care physician, a mental health provider specializing in children's needs, or a member of the clergy.

Monitor and Limit Your Family's Exposure to the Media

News coverage related to a disaster may elicit fear and confusion and arouse anxiety in children. This is particularly true for large-scale disasters or a terrorist event where significant property damage and loss of life has occurred. Particularly for younger children, repeated images of an event may cause them to believe the event is recurring over and over.

If parents allow children to watch television or use the Internet where images or news about the disaster are shown, parents should be with them to encourage communication and provide explanations. This may also include parent's monitoring and appropriately limiting their own exposure to anxiety-provoking information.

Use Support Networks

Parents help their children when they take steps to understand and manage their own feelings and ways of coping. They can do this by building and using social support systems of family, friends, community organizations and agencies, faith-based institutions, or other resources that work for that family. Parents can build their own unique social support systems so that in an emergency situation or when a disaster strikes, they can be supported and helped to manage their reactions. As a result, parents will be more available to their children and better able to support them. Parents are almost always the best source of support for children in difficult times. But to support their children, parents need to attend to their own needs and have a plan for their own support.

Preparing for disaster helps everyone in the family accept the fact that disasters do happen, and provides an opportunity to identify and collect the resources needed to meet basic needs after disaster. Preparation helps; when people feel prepared, they cope better and so do children.

Helping Others

The compassion and generosity of the American people is never more evident than after a disaster. People want to help. Here are some general guidelines on helping others after a disaster.

- Volunteer! Check with local organizations or listen to local news reports for information about where volunteers are needed. *Note:* Until volunteers are specifically requested, stay away from disaster areas.

- Bring your own food, water, and emergency supplies to a disaster area if you are needed there. This is especially important in cases where a large area has been affected and emergency items are in short supply.

- Donate to a recognized disaster relief organization. These groups are organized to purchase what is needed, and get it to the people who need it most.

- Do not drop off food, clothing, or any other item to a government agency or disaster relief organization unless a particular item has been requested. Normally, these organizations do not have the resources to sort through the donated items.

- Donate a quantity of a given item or class of items (such as nonperishable food) rather than a mix of different items. Determine where your donation is going, how it's going to get there, who is going to unload it, and how it is going to be distributed. Without sufficient planning, much-needed supplies will be left unused.

For More Information

If you require more information about any of these topics, the following are resources that may be helpful.

FEMA Publications

Helping Children Cope with Disasters. L-196. Provides information about how to prepare children for disaster and how to lessen the emotional effects of disaster.

When Disaster Strikes. L-217. Provides information about donations and volunteer organizations.

Repairing Your Flooded Home. FEMA 234. This 362-page publication provides a step-by-step guide to repairing your home and how to get help after a flood disaster. Available online at www.fema.gov/hazards/floods/lib234.shtm.

After a Flood: The First Steps. L 198. Tips for staying healthy, cleaning up and repairing, and getting help after a flood. Available online at www.fema.gov/hazards/floods/aftrfld.shtm.

APPENDIX A: WATER CONSERVATION TIPS

INDOOR WATER CONSERVATION TIPS

General

- Never pour water down the drain when there may be another use for it. Use it to water your indoor plants or garden.
- Repair dripping faucets by replacing washers. One drop per second wastes twenty-seven hundred gallons of water per year!
- Check all plumbing for leaks. Have leaks repaired by a plumber.
- Retrofit all household faucets by installing aerators with flow restrictors.
- Install an instant hot water heater on your sink.
- Insulate your water pipes to reduce heat loss and prevent them from breaking.
- Install a water-softening system only when the minerals in the water would damage your pipes. Turn the softener off while on vacation.
- Choose appliances that are more energy and water efficient.

Bathroom

- Consider purchasing a low-volume toilet that uses less than half the water of older models. Note: In many areas, low-volume units are required by law.
- Install a toilet displacement device to cut down on the amount of water needed to flush. Place a one-gallon plastic jug of water into the tank to displace toilet flow (do not use a brick, it may dissolve and loose pieces may cause damage to the internal parts). Be sure installation does not interfere with the operating parts.
- Replace your showerhead with an ultra-low-flow version.
- Place a bucket in the shower to catch excess water for watering plants.
- Avoid flushing the toilet unnecessarily. Dispose of tissues, insects, and other similar waste in the trash rather than the toilet.
- Avoid taking baths—take short showers—and turn on water only to get wet and lather and then again to rinse off.
- Avoid letting the water run while brushing your teeth, washing your face, or shaving.

Kitchen

- Operate automatic dishwashers only when they are fully loaded. Use the "light wash" feature, if available, to use less water.
- Hand wash dishes by filling two containers—one with soapy water and the other with rinse water containing a small amount of chlorine bleach.
- Clean vegetables in a pan filled with water rather than running water from the tap.
- Start a compost pile as an alternate method of disposing of food waste or simply dispose of food in the garbage. (Kitchen sink disposals require a lot of water to operate properly.)

- Store drinking water in the refrigerator. Do not let the tap run while you are waiting for water to cool.
- Avoid wasting water waiting for it to get hot. Capture it for other uses such as plant watering or heat it on the stove or in a microwave.
- Avoid rinsing dishes before placing them in the dishwasher; just remove large particles of food. (Most dishwashers can clean soiled dishes very well, so dishes do not have to be rinsed before washing.)
- Avoid using running water to thaw meat or other frozen foods. Defrost food overnight in the refrigerator or use the defrost setting on your microwave oven.

Laundry

- Operate automatic clothes washers only when they are fully loaded or set the water level for the size of your load.

OUTDOOR WATER CONSERVATION TIPS

General

- Check your well pump periodically. If the automatic pump turns on and off while water is not being used, you have a leak.
- Plant native and/or drought-tolerant grasses, ground covers, shrubs, and trees. Once established, they do not need water as frequently and usually will survive a dry period without watering. Small plants require less water to become established. Group plants together based on similar water needs.
- Install irrigation devices that are the most water efficient for each use. Micro and drip irrigation and soaker hoses are examples of efficient devices.
- Use mulch to retain moisture in the soil. Mulch also helps control weeds that compete with landscape plants for water.

- Avoid purchasing recreational water toys that require a constant stream of water.
- Avoid installing ornamental water features (such as fountains) unless they use recycled water.

Car Washing

- Use a shut-off nozzle that can be adjusted down to a fine spray on your hose.
- Use a commercial car wash that recycles water. If you wash your own car, park on the grass so that you will be watering it at the same time.

Lawn Care

- Avoid overwatering your lawn. A heavy rain eliminates the need for watering for up to two weeks. Most of the year, lawns only need one inch of water per week.
- Water in several short sessions rather than one long one, in order for your lawn to better absorb moisture.
- Position sprinklers so water lands on the lawn and shrubs and not on paved areas.
- Avoid sprinklers that spray a fine mist. Mist can evaporate before it reaches the lawn. Check sprinkler systems and timing devices regularly to be sure they operate properly.
- Raise the lawn mower blade to at least three inches or to its highest level. A higher cut encourages grass roots to grow deeper, shades the root system, and holds soil moisture.
- Plant drought-resistant lawn seed.
- Avoid overfertilizing your lawn. Applying fertilizer increases the need for water. Apply fertilizers that contain slow-release, water-insoluble forms of nitrogen.
- Use a broom or blower instead of a hose to clean leaves and other debris from your driveway or sidewalk.

- Avoid leaving sprinklers or hoses unattended. A garden hose can pour out six hundred gallons or more in only a few hours.

Pool

- Install a new water-saving pool filter. A single back flushing with a traditional filter uses 180 to 250 gallons of water.
- Cover pools and spas to reduce evaporation of water.

APPENDIX B: DISASTER SUPPLIES CHECKLIST

The following list is to help you determine what to include in your disaster supplies kit that will meet your family's needs.

FIRST-AID SUPPLIES HOME (H) VEHICLE (V) WORK (W)

_____ Adhesive bandages, various sizes

_____ Five-by-nine-inch sterile dressing

_____ Conforming roller gauze bandage

_____ Triangular bandages

_____ Three-by-three-inch sterile gauze pads

_____ Four-by-four-inch sterile gauze pads

_____ Roll three-inch cohesive bandage

_____ Germicidal hand wipes or waterless, alcohol-based hand sanitizer

_____ Antiseptic wipes

_____ Pairs large, medical-grade, nonlatex gloves

_____ Tongue depressor blades

_____ Adhesive tape, two-inch width

_____ Antibacterial ointment

_____ Cold pack

_____ Scissors (small, personal)

_____ Tweezers

_____ Assorted sizes of safety pins

_____ Cotton balls

_____ Thermometer

_____ Tube of petroleum jelly or other lubricant

_____ Sunscreen

_____ CPR breathing barrier, such as a face shield

_____ First-aid manual

NONPRESCRIPTION AND PRESCRIPTION MEDICINE KIT SUPPLIES HOME (H) VEHICLE (V) WORK (W)

_____ Aspirin and nonaspirin pain reliever

_____ Antidiarrhea medication

_____ Antacid (for stomach upset)

_____ Laxative

_____ Vitamins

_____ Prescriptions

_____ Extra eyeglasses/contact lenses

SANITATION AND HYGIENE SUPPLIES HOME (H) VEHICLE (V) WORK (W)

_____ Washcloth and towel

_____ Towelettes, soap, hand sanitizer

_____ Toothpaste, toothbrushes

_____ Shampoo, comb, and brush

_____ Deodorants, sunscreen

_____ Razor, shaving cream

_____ Lip balm, insect repellent

_____ Contact lens solutions

_____ Mirror

_____ Feminine supplies

_____ Heavy-duty plastic garbage bags and ties for personal sanitation uses and toilet paper

_____ Medium-sized plastic bucket with tight lid

_____ Disinfectant and household chlorine bleach

_____ A small shovel for digging a latrine

_____ Toilet paper

EQUIPMENT AND TOOLS HOME (H) VEHICLE (V) WORK (W)

_____ Portable, battery-powered radio or television and extra batteries

_____ NOAA Weather Radio, if appropriate for your area

_____ Flashlight and extra batteries

_____ Signal flare

_____ Matches in a waterproof container (or waterproof matches)

_____ Shut-off wrench, pliers, shovel, and other tools

_____ Duct tape and scissors

_____ Plastic sheeting

_____ Whistle

_____ Small canister, ABC-type fire extinguisher

_____ Tube tent

_____ Compass

_____ Work gloves

_____ Paper, pens, and pencils

_____ Needles and thread

_____ Battery-operated travel alarm clock

KITCHEN ITEMS HOME (H) VEHICLE (V) WORK (W)

_____ Manual can opener

_____ Mess kits or paper cups, plates, and plastic utensils

_____ All-purpose knife

_____ Household liquid bleach to treat drinking water

_____ Sugar, salt, pepper

_____ Aluminum foil and plastic wrap

_____ Resealable plastic bags

_____ Small cooking stove and a can of cooking fuel (if food must be cooked)

COMFORT ITEMS HOME (H) VEHICLE (V) WORK (W)

_____ Games

_____ Cards

_____ Books

_____ Toys for kids

_____ Foods

FOOD AND WATER HOME (H) VEHICLE (V) WORK (W)

_____ Water

_____ Ready-to-eat meats, fruits, and vegetables

_____ Canned or boxed juices, milk, and soup

_____ High-energy foods such as peanut butter, jelly, low-sodium crackers, granola bars, and trail mix

_____ Vitamins

_____ Special foods for infants or persons on special diets

_____ Cookies, hard candy

_____ Instant coffee

_____ Cereals

_____ Powdered milk

CLOTHES AND BEDDING SUPPLIES HOME (H) VEHICLE (V) WORK (W)

_____ Complete change of clothes

_____ Sturdy shoes or boots

_____ Rain gear

_____ Hat and gloves

_____ Extra socks

_____ Extra underwear

_____ Thermal underwear

_____ Sunglasses

_____ Blankets/sleeping bags and pillows

DOCUMENTS AND KEYS* HOME (H) VEHICLE (V) WORK (W)

_____ Personal identification

_____ Cash and coins

_____ Credit cards

_____ Extra set of house keys and car keys

_____ Copies of the following:

_____ Birth certificate

_____ Marriage certificate

_____ Driver's license

_____ Social Security cards

_____ Passports

_____ Wills

_____ Deeds

_____ Inventory of household goods

_____ Insurance papers

_____ Immunization records

_____ Bank and credit card account numbers

_____ Stocks and bonds

_____ Emergency contact list and phone numbers

_____ Map of the area and phone numbers of places you could go

Make sure you keep these items in a watertight container.

APPENDIX C: FAMILY COMMUNICATIONS PLAN

 Homeland Security **Family Communications Plan**

Your family may not be together when disaster strikes, so plan how you will contact one another and review what you will do in different situations.

Out-of-State Contact Name: _____ Telephone Number: _____
Email: _____ Telephone Number: _____

Fill out the following information for each family member and keep it up to date.

Name: _____ Social Security Number: _____
Date of Birth: _____ Important Medical Information: _____

Name: _____ Social Security Number: _____
Date of Birth: _____ Important Medical Information: _____

Name: _____ Social Security Number: _____
Date of Birth: _____ Important Medical Information: _____

Name: _____ Social Security Number: _____
Date of Birth: _____ Important Medical Information: _____

Name: _____ Social Security Number: _____
Date of Birth: _____ Important Medical Information: _____

Name: _____ Social Security Number: _____
Date of Birth: _____ Important Medical Information: _____

Where to go in an emergency. Write down where your family spends the most time: work, school and other places you frequent. Schools, daycare providers, workplaces and apartment buildings should all have site-specific emergency plans.

Home
Address: _____
Phone Number: _____
Neighborhood Meeting Place: _____
Regional Meeting Place: _____

Work
Address: _____
Phone Number: _____
Evacuation Location: _____

School
Address: _____
Phone Number: _____
Evacuation Location: _____

Work
Address: _____
Phone Number: _____
Evacuation Location: _____

School
Address: _____
Phone Number: _____
Evacuation Location: _____

Other place you frequent:
Address: _____
Phone Number: _____
Evacuation Location: _____

School
Address: _____
Phone Number: _____
Evacuation Location: _____

Other place you frequent:
Address: _____
Phone Number: _____
Evacuation Location: _____

Important Information	Name	Telephone #	Policy #
Doctor(s):			
Other:			
Pharmacist:			
Medical Insurance:			
Homeowners/Rental Insurance:			
Veterinarian/Kennel (for pets):			

Other useful phone numbers: 9-1-1 for emergencies. Police Non-Emergency Phone #: _____

Every family member should carry a copy of this important information:

Other Important Phone Numbers & Information:

Family Communications Plan

Contact Name:

Telephone:

Out-of-State Contact Name:

Telephone:

Neighborhood Meeting Place:

Meeting Place Telephone:

Dial 9–1–1 for Emergencies!

Other Important Phone Numbers & Information:

Family Communications Plan

Contact Name:

Telephone:

Out-of-State Contact Name:

Telephone:

Neighborhood Meeting Place:

Meeting Place Telephone:

Dial 9–1–1 for Emergencies!

FOLD HERE

Other Important Phone Numbers & Information:

Family Communications Plan

Contact Name:

Telephone:

Out-of-State Contact Name:

Telephone:

Neighborhood Meeting Place:

Meeting Place Telephone:

Dial 9–1–1 for Emergencies!

Other Important Phone Numbers & Information:

Family Communications Plan

Contact Name:

Telephone:

Out-of-State Contact Name:

Telephone:

Neighborhood Meeting Place:

Meeting Place Telephone:

Dial 9–1–1 for Emergencies!